20p

Coping

with Angina

Coping with Angina

Practical advice to help you
lead an active, pain-free life

Louise M. Wallace with Christine Bundy

THORSONS PUBLISHING GROUP

First published 1990

British Library Cataloguing in Publication Data

Coping with angina.
  1. Man. Heart. Angina pectoris. Therapy. Self-help
  I. Wallace, Louise   II. Bundy, Christine
  616.12206

  ISBN 0-7225-2183-9

Published by Thorsons Publishers Limited, Wellingborough, Northants NN8 2RQ, England

Typeset by Harper Phototypesetters Ltd, Northampton, England

Printed in Great Britain by Mackays of Chatham, Kent

10 9 8 7 6 5 4 3 2 1

Contributors

South Birmingham Angina Research Group:
Louise M. Wallace, Top Grade Clinical Psychologist
(Physical Health)

Christine Bundy, Research Psychologist

Charlotte Carrington, Senior Physiotherapist

South Birmingham Coronary Prevention Group:
Paul Bennett, Senior Clinical Psychologist

Michael Clapham, Senior Dietitian

Contributor and Medical Advisor
Robert Davies, Senior Registrar in Physical
Medicine, Dundee Royal Infirmary

Contents

Introduction

If you have angina, or someone close to you has angina, or if you are a health-care professional who works with people with angina, you will know that angina is a sign of a serious heart condition, and anything that threatens the heart threatens life itself. But people with angina *do* live to a ripe old age, and most will eventually die of some other cause. There *is* life with angina!

Angina is a sign of heart disease, but does *not* directly threaten life itself. Chapter 1 examines what angina is, its causes and symptoms. It spells out the possible role that lifestyle may have had in leading to heart disease, and the even harder evidence that how you live now, when you smoke, take exercise, what you eat, and how stressed you are, can influence your future health and well-being. But before you safely make changes to these things for yourself, it is important that you understand and get the best out of your medical care. There have been many advances in the diagnosis and treatment of heart disease, as described in Chapter 2.

Where does this new lifestyle approach to angina come from?

In 1983, a young cardiologist, Dean Ornish, and his team published an astonishing paper in a prestigious medical journal, *The Journal of the American Heart Association*. He compared one set of 23 patients with another 23 who were matched for the severity of their angina. He gave the first group an intensive programme of relaxation and a strict low-fat diet for two weeks. He gave them various tests of their mental and physical health. He showed that there were significant improvements in the group of patients given a special relaxation and diet programme compared to the matched patients. They felt more relaxed and some had given up smoking. But more impressive still, the heart function tests during exercise showed that even in this short time their hearts were more efficient, and the patients themselves reported less severe and less frequent angina.[1]

Now, Dr Ornish was fortunate in being able to give these people their treatment in a 5-star country club! But the results were so impressive it spurred a group of staff in the British National Health Service to form a South Birmingham Angina Research Group. We decided to see if two methods of lifestyle change – stress management training, including relaxation, and exercise training – would have similar effects. The main difference from the Ornish study was that all patients were seen in an ordinary hospital outpatient department, and they attended for classes over a seven-week period. Our early results of a study of 120 people with severe angina over four years show that both methods produce beneficial effects for most sufferers. Most people are very highly satisfied with these methods and feel more in control of their disease and of their future. But, more dramatically, the patients are able to take more exercise and have less chest pain; these effects were still noticeable three months after they had left the programme. Many have now joined the South Birmingham Angina Support Group for mutual support, as described in Chapter 11.

Very recent research by Dr Ornish suggests that even more dramatic effects may occur if people with angina make major changes in their overall lifestyle, including not only stress management and exercise, but also diet and smoking. In a new study about to be published, Ornish has tested the idea that lifestyle change can actually reverse some of the physical effects of the disease. He claims that in some people, there is evidence that severely blocked heart blood vessels which cause angina have become *less* blocked and these patients can do more exercise and have less chest pain than people who have had routine medical care. It may be many years before we know whether these results are reliable. It will be longer before we know whether every person with angina needs to make the very drastic changes in lifestyle suggested, and it may be even longer still before we know whether less dramatic changes are sufficient for most people. But these early results are promising enough for us to encourage you to be prepared to make changes in how you handle stress (Chapters 3, 4, 5, 6, 7), exercise (Chapter 8) as well as smoking (Chapter 9) and your diet (Chapter 10).

How to use this book

The first two chapters will help you to understand what angina is, how it is diagnosed and treated, and how you can get the best out of the health-care system. The remaining chapters offer you information on why lifestyle change may influence your heart, how to assess your vulnerability and strengths, how to make changes and how to monitor your progress.

Generally, it is better to make one major change, for example, in your smoking habits, before moving on to another, such as your diet, rather than all at once. You may feel overburdened by the short-term 'costs' of change, such as nicotine withdrawal from smoking, and aches and pains from unaccustomed exercise, before you reap the long-term benefits of being smoke-free, fitter, more relaxed and enjoying a healthy diet. So that is why it is sensible to read the book right through at first, then go back and take the most important chapters for you one at a time.

Show the book to your family and friends to let them know what you are aiming to do for yourself. Many people with angina complain that people do not understand them, or they are too protective. It is important you know your disease, your symptoms and your capabilities so that you can learn to help yourself. But as other people cannot read your mind, and cannot see your angina pain, it is important you get in the habit of asking for help when you need it. Then when you do not need help, people can see you are able to get on with it yourself!

Finally, a vote of thanks

We wish to thank Dr Robert E. Nagle, Consultant Cardiologist, for unfailing support for the research, and for his continued medical care of the people with angina in South Birmingham. We thank the Mental Health Foundation, British Heart Foundation and the Chest, Heart and Stroke Association for supporting our research. Last but not least, we thank the people with angina without whose enthusiasm and personal experience this book would not have been written. We have every confidence that you, the reader, will benefit as much as our patients from this new approach to caring for your heart. In partnership with the best of medical care, your heart and health are in your hands!

CHAPTER 1

What is angina?

In order to help you understand why angina occurs, we need to look at the workings of the heart and blood vessels and at the common diseases which affect them. The causes of heart disease will be discussed, and those over which you have most control in your daily life will be introduced in preparation for subsequent chapters. Angina is the pain that is experienced when the heart muscle cannot get enough oxygen to cope with the task it is being asked to do. It is the heart's way of saying 'slow down, I'm struggling here!' In order to understand angina better it helps to know more about the heart, and especially the blood vessels associated with it.

The heart

The heart is a hollow, muscular pump about the size of a large

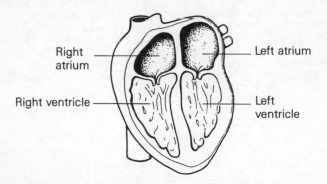

Right atrium

Left atrium

Right ventricle

Left ventricle

Fig 1: The chambers of the heart

clenched fist. It is situated in the centre of the chest with the bottom end lying slightly towards the left side. The heart walls are made up of a special type of muscle which contracts rhythmically and, unlike the muscles in our legs and arms, it does not tire. The inside is made up of four chambers, two smaller ones at the top called atria (sing. atrium) and two larger ones at the bottom called ventricles. The chambers are divided by valves which control the flow of blood through them. This blood flow is strictly regulated and usually occurs only in one direction. The heart receives used blood from the body, pumping it to the lungs to collect oxygen and remove carbon dioxide and also to collect fresh blood from the lungs to pump around the vital organs, nourishing them. It is the sound of the valves opening and closing that your doctor will be listening for when examining your chest with a stethoscope. Each heartbeat consists of the two top chambers (atria) filling with blood and the bottom two chambers (ventricles) expelling the blood, which makes the characteristic 'lub-dub' sound.

The blood pressure

The blood is being pumped from the heart to the blood vessels

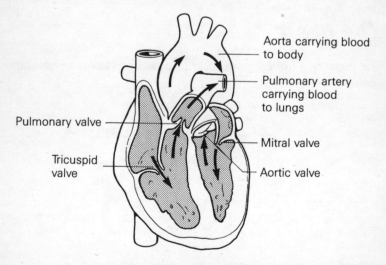

Fig 2: The flow of blood through the heart

under pressure to allow it to reach all parts of the body. This pressure will vary between people and within each person depending on circumstances. The circumstances within the body which maintain the pressure include the amount of blood being pumped through the heart chambers and the degree of resistance in the vessels through which it flows. So, if the vessel is wide and clear, the pressure will be lower than if the vessel is narrowed or constricted, which is what can occur with heart disease. Hard exercise or stress can also cause a rise in the blood pressure.

The coronary arteries

The heart has to have its own supply of oxygen-rich blood in order to perform its task of beating continuously throughout life. The blood vessels which supply the heart with this blood are called the *coronary arteries*. There are two main arteries, right and left, which encircle the heart, subdividing into many smaller connecting branches called the collateral system. The left artery is the larger of the two. This left artery divides into two main branches which is why doctors talk of there being three coronary arteries. These are named the right coronary artery, the left circumflex artery and the left anterior descending artery. The

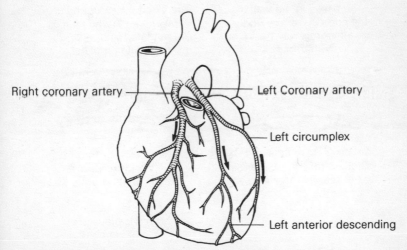

Fig 3: The coronary arteries

heart muscle is covered with arteries which supply it with the much-needed blood and oxygen, its energy source (see Fig 3).

Heart disease

There are many forms of heart disease: some may be present from birth such as rare malformations of the structure of the heart, and others take a lifetime to acquire. The more common acquired heart diseases are the subject of this book. From about the time of our early 20s fatty deposits called atheroma, which are made by our body, begin to stick to the artery walls so they start to become thickened and less elastic. This silting-up process can continue for many years without giving rise to symptoms; in some people, it never causes a medical crisis and is only discovered after death, at post-mortem. However, for a large proportion of people this process can cause major problems, usually about the time of middle age. See Fig 4.

Coronary disease is the umbrella term for a narrowing of the coronary arteries due to a buildup of atheroma. The other names

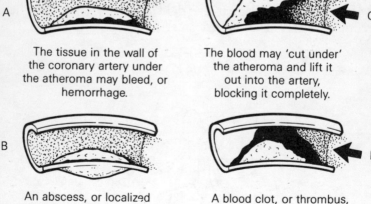

A

The tissue in the wall of the coronary artery under the atheroma may bleed, or hemorrhage.

C

The blood may 'cut under' the atheroma and lift it out into the artery, blocking it completely.

B

An abscess, or localized infection, may form in the wall of the coronary artery under the atheroma.

D

A blood clot, or thrombus, often forms over or around an atheroma. The term 'coronary thrombosis' means that the coronary artery is blocked by a blood clot.

Fig 4: Atheroma in the coronary artery

for it include atherosclerosis, coronary heart disease, ischaemic heart disease and coronary artery disease. The main consequences of this disease are angina and heart attack.

Who gets coronary disease?

Coronary disease affects about 1,000,000 people in the United Kingdom every year. It mainly affects men but women also develop it: the ratio of men to women is about 4 to 1. The reason for this is that women up to the age of the menopause are partially protected by their natural supply of hormones, mainly oestrogen. But as this supply decreases during and after the menopause, the protection wears off. After this time, late middle age, the numbers of women who develop coronary heart disease equals that of men. The symptoms of the disease usually become apparent in middle age although it is not uncommon for a young man, or even a young woman, with no obvious signs of heart disease to have heart disease from age 21 onwards.

What causes coronary disease?

When doctors assess the causes of coronary disease, of which

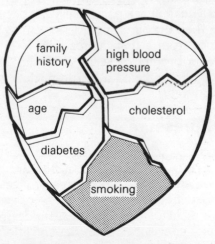

Fig 5: Causes of coronary disease

there are at least six main ones, they talk about 'risk factors'. Possessing one or more of these risk factors will increase your chances of developing coronary disease and carefully evaluating these risk factors can help doctors predict who in the general population will be most at risk of having a heart attack.

Lifestyle

It is said that coronary disease is the product of the lifestyle we lead in the Western world. Countries such as Japan, Czechoslovakia and Israel have a relatively low death rate from coronary disease but New Zealand, the USA, England and Wales have a much higher rate, and Finland and Scotland have very high rates, occupying first and fourth positions respectively in this league table of deaths. The way of life of a peasant in one of the poorer parts of the world is obviously very different from that of a city dweller in England or the USA. Food is less available and expensive food such as red meat is a rare delicacy. Hard physical exercise is a part of life in poor communities and stress in the form that we experience is unusual. Cigarette smoking used to be much commoner among more affluent people but the level of consumption, even in underdeveloped countries, is increasing all the time.

Family history

Coronary disease tends to run in families. If one member of your family has had a heart attack particularly if it occurred in his/her younger years, then the other members seem to be at risk. The main risk comes from a first degree relative – that is, one of your parents or a brother or sister. If a number of these first degree relatives have suffered a heart attack, then your risk is increased accordingly.

High blood pressure

When we are active, excited, or under stress, our blood pressure will go up automatically to supply extra blood and oxygen to the muscles and organs. High blood pressure, or hypertension, however, is a sustained high level of pressure even during rest. This is a major risk factor for heart disease and strokes. It is a very common disease in developed countries and affects about 20 per cent of the adult population in Britain today. High pressure in the artery walls puts a strain on the delicate lining, increasing the risk of some weaknesses occurring and accelerating the atheroma or silting-up process. Hypertension can affect any part of the body, but more usually it affects the brain in the form of a stroke, or the heart in the form of hypertensive heart disease. Being male, middle-aged or older, having a family history of hypertension, living a sedentary life and being under stress are the biggest factors in the risk of developing hypertension in the first instance, but once the disease has developed it can cause other complications such as heart disease.

High cholesterol

The level of fats or lipids in the blood is one of the most important risk factors in heart disease and the higher the levels the greater the risk. There are two main types of fats, cholesterol and triglycerides, both of which are made by the liver and are essential for life. One type of cholesterol, HDL cholesterol (HDL stands for High Density Lipoprotein), may be protective but LDL cholesterol (Low Density Lipoprotein) may increase the risk of thrombosis. These fats are transported around the body via the bloodstream to be used in maintaining the body. Taking a cholesterol-rich diet from which these fats can be absorbed and/or making too much of the wrong sort can cause the excessive fats to deposit themselves along the artery walls. This is especially dangerous in the small coronary arteries which can become blocked very easily. A high level of triglyceride is less common but can occur in people who are overweight, people with diabetes and people who take excessive sugar and alcohol. Having high blood lipids (fats) puts someone at risk of developing coronary disease as well as multiplying the importance of other risk factors they might have.

Smoking

The direct effects of smoking on heart disease are undeniable. Smoking is probably the single most important risk factor in heart disease because unlike cholesterol or blood pressure it is not necessary for maintaining life, and stopping smoking can produce a dramatic decrease in the risk of developing heart disease. Smoking also contributes to the risk of a heart attack occurring earlier in life, and increases one's chances of not surviving a heart attack.

Cigar and pipe-smokers have a reduced risk of developing heart disease, but their risk is still well above that of someone who doesn't smoke at all.

Smoking affects the heart by the action of nicotine and carbon monoxide. Nicotine stimulates adrenalin, the stress hormone, which suddenly increases the heart rate and blood pressure. The stress response is discussed more fully in Chapter 6. Carbon monoxide interferes with the ability of the blood to carry oxygen to the heart. The lasting effect of smoking is a combination of the effects of nicotine and carbon monoxide which stimulates the fatty deposit production, causes the blood to become sticky and therefore promotes the production and formation of a blood clot or *coronary thrombosis*.

Lack of exercise

Over the last 30 or 40 years our working and home life has changed dramatically. People now do less physically demanding work, homes have many labour-saving devices such as automatic washing machines and vacuum cleaners, and the majority of people own a car. As a result of all this, unless we seek exercise for exercise's sake, many weeks can go by without us experiencing significant physical exertion. There is now a great deal of evidence from well-conducted research studies to show that those people who do less physically are more at risk of developing heart disease than those who exercise regularly. In fact, those who exercise regularly have a lower death rate from all causes than their sedentary contemporaries.

Regular aerobic exercise, that is the sort that trains your heart and lungs, for a minimum of 20 minutes per session, three to four times a week, is all that is required to lower the risk of developing heart disease. This is discussed more fully in Chapter 8.

There are many benefits from exercise. It can help to lower the blood pressure, help to control weight and it has the effect of calming and building confidence.

Diabetes

People who have diabetes are more likely to develop heart disease than people who don't have diabetes. This book will not cover the reasons why, but will concentrate more on those risk factors that you can do something about.

Stress

Stress is a highly complex and personal matter. It has been shown to contribute to both heart attacks (Jenkins, 1976)[1] and angina (Medalie *et al*, 1973),[2] but because it is difficult to measure stress, to what extent it contributes is not known exactly. How it is linked to heart disease is discussed here, although the following chapters describe stress in more detail.

Stress and heart attack

When people who have experienced a heart attack are asked what they think the cause of it was, most people will implicate stress in some way. Research supports that some types of stress have been shown to be associated with an increased incidence of coronary disease. This is not the same as saying stress causes heart attacks, however. There are three main areas of stress which have connections with heart attacks. These are work stress, home stress and personal style.

Work stress

Changing jobs frequently has been linked with heart attacks, as has shift work and low activity at work (Sales, 1969).[3] However, it is not just the negative aspects of work which are harmful. Positive events, such as a recent promotion, can also have effects.

Domestic stress

The most consistent type of home stress which is linked with heart disease is the loss of a partner, either through death (Parkes *et al*, 1969)[4] or divorce. Also, many large changes such as moving job and home, perhaps the birth of a child and/or death of a close relative, if occurring together have been associated with heart attacks. More about these in Chapter 4.

Personal style

There is now a good deal of evidence which links the way we behave with heart disease. Recently, research has shown that more people of a character called Type A are likely to have heart disease than those of another type, called Type B. Type A is the behaviour pattern or set of characteristics which include being preoccupied with time, constantly running to deadlines, being overcompetitive, being hostile and aggressive and having a strong sense of achievement drive. Behaving in this way has been shown to be a risk factor for heart disease (Cooper, 1981).[5] More about this in Chapter 5.

Stress and angina

The research on stress and angina is not so extensive as that on stress and heart attacks. However, we do know that experimentally-induced psychological stress can result in a decreased blood supply to the heart muscle possibly through coronary spasm (Deanfield *et al*, 1974).[5] Coronary spasm is a form of cramp in the very small coronary arteries. There is good evidence from special X-rays taken during these experiments which show people with angina having 'silent angina' attacks, and even people with normal coronary arteries can show this lack of blood supply in response to stress. Silent angina or *ischaemia* is evidence of coronary spasm but without the associated pain in the heart.

How does stress contribute to heart attack and angina?

Stress signals are received and interpreted by the brain which responds by producing chemicals which stimulate the production of other chemicals in other parts of the body. This pattern of responses is complicated and involves most of the systems in the body including the heart and blood system. The extent of the response to stress will depend on the degree of threat to the individual, and whether it is a new type of stress or whether the person has dealt with it before. The consequences of that response will depend on the degree of response and the general state of health of the system under attack. A small stressor to a healthy person may not have great consequences, but an unfamiliar and large stressor to a person with angina may have damaging effects.

   The stress hormones that are released during threat are known to increase blood pressure and stimulate coronary spasm, angina, silent ischaemia and even heart attacks in some instances. The precise effects of stressful stimuli on the various body systems is described in greater detail in Chapter 6.

What is a heart attack?

The medical name for a heart attack is *myocardial infarction* and like most medical terms it tells you what happens but not why it happens. The myocardium is the layer of special muscle which the heart is made up of and which keeps the heart beating. Infarction means scarring; therefore, myocardial infarction literally means 'scarred heart muscle'. You may also hear people talk of a 'coronary' or 'coronary thrombosis'. All of these terms usually add up to the same thing, a *heart attack*.

A heart attack usually presents itself as a medical emergency. The person may have extreme symptoms of pain and/or breathlessness, nausea and possibly loss of consciousness, which will cause the person to need medical help. However, some heart attacks may go unnoticed at the time and may only show up as such on future examination of the heart. This is termed 'silent myocardial infarction'.

A heart attack is a sudden and dramatic interruption to the supply of blood (and therefore oxygen) to the heart muscle via the coronary arteries. This occurs because the artery becomes blocked either by 'a clot' or *thrombus*, or because the artery goes into spasm long enough to cut off the blood supply completely.

Muscle without a fresh supply of blood can only survive for a short time, as little as one or two hours, before irreversible changes occur and the muscle dies. Once an area of heart

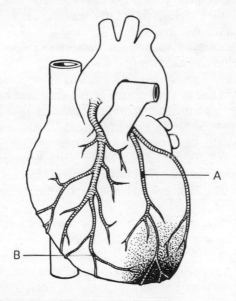

Fig 6: Location of heart attacks: A – serious; B – less serious

muscle is destroyed, a scar forms around it just like a scar in any other part of the body. The amount of heart muscle that dies and scars can vary from a microscopically small area to a very extensive area. When the latter occurs, it is possible that the person will not survive the attack. The deciding factor in this is the extent of involvement and where the blockage occurs. If a blockage occurs in the left anterior descending coronary artery (see A in Fig 6) then a very large area of heart will be damaged. If a blockage occurs in a minor branch of the right coronary artery (see B in Fig 6), on the other hand, then it will have much less serious consequences.

The second serious consequence of a heart attack is a disturbance of the heart's normal pumping rhythm. If a blockage occurs near the position in the heart of the natural pacemaker (a collection of nerve fibres which regulate the heartbeat) or if a large enough area of myocardium is damaged, then the electrical timing of the heart can be severely, even fatally, disrupted.

The symptoms of a heart attack

Some people mistakenly believe that a heart attack means that their heart has stopped. This is not the case. However, if the heart attack is serious enough then it can cause the heart to stop, and this is called a *cardiac arrest*.

The symptoms may vary from person to person, but they typically involve the following:

Pain: This may range from a dull ache to a very severe vice-like pain, usually in the central chest, but it may also radiate down the left arm, up into the throat and down as far as the abdomen.

Breathlessness: Shortness of breath, shallow breathing, or a gasping for breath, may be due to the heart attack itself or can occur because of heightened anxiety or fright associated with the feelings of pain and the thoughts of possible death. It is the perfectly understandable reaction to such a major threat to one's life.

Nausea: Again, this symptom may or may not be present or it can actually cause some people to vomit.

Dizziness: Lightheadedness, dizziness and even loss of consciousness are sometimes experienced, and should never be ignored because they are serious signs of heart attack.

Because people are so different there are many different reactions in the way we feel, think and behave regarding a heart attack. The above symptoms are typical but not everyone will have the typical symptoms. This may be one of the reasons your doctor may at first be unsure about the diagnosis of heart attack. Someone who regularly has angina may think it is just another angina attack and some people have no symptoms at all and are unaware that they have had a heart attack.

Medical treatment of heart attack

Once a heart attack is suspected, the doctor will usually admit you to a Coronary Care Unit to enable more extensive observation of the signs and symptoms. The *signs* are the medical indications of the illness, which the patient may not be aware of, whereas the *symptoms* are the things the patient may complain of. The symptoms of a heart attack have been described above. The signs that the doctor in this case will be looking for are fluctuations in the heart rhythm or rate, and fluctuations in blood pressure which correspond to the ability of the heart to pump the required amount of blood around the body. In order to check for these abnormalities, the doctor will request some tests such as blood tests for cardiac damage. The blood will also reveal the chemicals that are released when the heart attack has occurred. Other tests which may be done are electrocardiogram (ECG) and blood pressure recordings. These tests will be explained in greater detail in the next chapter. Drugs that control pain or sedate people may be used to prevent the extra strain on the heart if someone is distressed, frightened or in severe pain. Once the diagnosis has been confirmed, usually by ECG evidence, and the blood test results indicate a heart attack has occurred, the person will be confined to bed for up to 48 hours initially, and then gradually encouraged to return to everyday life.

After discharge from the hospital, the doctor will advise gradual resumption of all activities unless the person is limited by pain or by further symptoms. It is extremely difficult to give people specific advice on what they should or should not do, because there are great differences between people in their level of fitness, the extent of their heart attack and their ability to cope psychologically with the event. Most people will feel anxious and some will feel depressed after being at home for some time. It is normal to feel apprehensive and concerned about the future. This will, however, pass and most people overcome their fears and go on to make a full recovery.

What is angina?

Angina is the common type of coronary disease. About 1,000,000 middle-aged men in the UK have angina (Fox, 1988).[7]

Angina pectoris is the medical name for the pain that some people with coronary disease experience. It is caused by an imbalance in the oxygen supply and demand to the coronary arteries. As previously discussed, the heart needs a good supply of blood and, therefore, oxygen, to continue beating. When the arteries are diseased they are narrowed and therefore cannot give the required amount of oxygen. A normal heart could cope with an almost unlimited demand for oxygen. When the heart does not receive adequate oxygen it gives out a warning pain: this is the angina. It indicates that the heart has reached its maximum workload and cannot respond to increased demand, and so the muscle is temporarily starved of oxygen. Angina pain in itself is not usually harmful to the muscle because most people have to rest when they experience it and the muscle receives blood again. However, angina is unfortunately a symptom of the underlying heart disease which is slowly progressing.

What triggers angina?

The walls of normal coronary arteries are smooth, clean and elastic. This allows them to contract and expand to give more oxygen and blood to the heart when it is required, to cope with any extra demand. This extra demand may come from a number of sources: for example, when the body is working harder, climbing a hill, running for a bus, doing strenuous housework; when the body is under stress or fighting an infection; when we have to deal with excessive emotion, for example, rage, fear, anxiety; or when the vessels themselves cause problems, as in coronary spasm, then the heart receives extra electrical stimulation via the nerves to make it pump more blood around the body. In order to do this the coronary arteries have to supply more blood and oxygen to the heart itself.

The healthy heart can cope with these extra demands. However, coronary disease results in the lining of the arteries becoming thicker, therefore narrower in diameter, and less elastic. This means that when extra demand is placed on the heart, the coronary arteries cannot respond effectively and not enough oxygen gets through. This is known as the *oxygen deficit*.

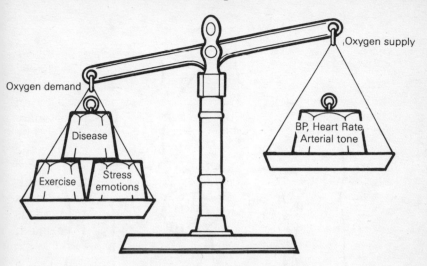

Fig 7: The oxygen deficit

When people become familiar with their angina, they learn what events trigger off the pain. Some of the most common triggers are:

Smoking, physical exertion: Running, lifting and carrying heavy loads – especially first thing in the morning or after a heavy meal – walking in cold winds or very hot climates.

Stress: Anger, anxiety, fright, arguments, talking in public or complaining about a purchase.

These triggers are very individual and some people will respond more to the physical triggers than the psychological ones and vice versa.

The symptoms of angina

As with the symptoms of a heart attack, the symptoms of angina will vary both from person to person and from attack to attack. The typical symptoms are as follows:

Pain

This is usually described as a heavy, gripping pain in the centre of the chest just behind the breast bone. It can radiate down one or both arms and to the throat, neck and jaws. The heart does not have its own nerve supply and so it uses the nerve pathways of neighbouring structures. This is known as *referred pain*. This pain can feel different to different people: it can range from a

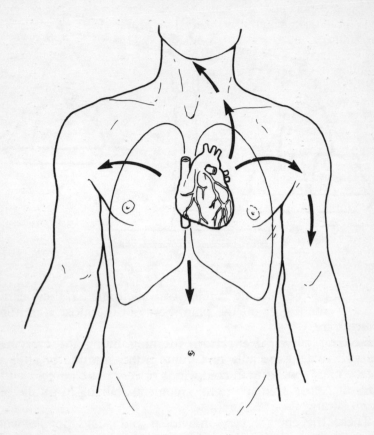

Fig 8: Angina pain. Arrows indicate where pain typically radiates to

mild ache or discomfort similar to pins and needles in the chest, arm, shoulder, back or jaw, to a severe central pain which resembles the description of a heart attack. Some people have been found to experience angina pains in their fingers, knees and toes. Experiencing severe pain does not necessarily mean you have more coronary disease, it simply means you experience more pain than someone else. Because angina pain is so different in different people, it can be mistaken for indigestion or heartburn, rheumatism, trapped nerves or general muscular complaints. For this reason your doctor may not always diagnose it as angina until it becomes more obvious.

Breathlessness
For some people this is the most obvious symptom. Shortness

of breath and a choking sensation can come on at any time but it is more usual when it is related to exercise, especially walking up stairs or hills. At some time almost everyone with angina will experience it whilst resting or in bed – some people have been known to wake up from a dream about running or a nightmare with angina. For most people it is more predictable and, given time, most people can learn when their angina is likely to begin.

Usually breathlessness occurs before the pain, but for some people this is the only symptom they experience. It typically lasts for a couple of minutes and then passes off providing the person stops what he/she is doing and rests.

Heavy limbs

A symptom which is not often associated with angina, but one which people who have the disease say is very common and can be troublesome, is that of heaviness or deadness in one or all of their limbs. The left arm is the most usual site of this discomfort, but when both are involved, carrying out routine daily activities such as shopping or cleaning can prove extremely difficult. One man with angina has termed this the 'diver's boots' syndrome.

Fatigue

Like the other vague symptoms of heavy limbs, some people experience fatigue a great deal. Some people say it is not always present, but occasionally it can be present on getting up in the morning to last thing at night. It may only last one day or it may occur for two to three days at a time. The feature which makes this aspect of angina frustrating is its unpredictability. Although it can be triggered off by doing too much the previous day, sometimes it seems to occur for no apparent reason.

The different types of angina

There are two main types of angina. The first is called *chronic stable angina* or *angina of effort* and is the most common type. The second is less common and occurs at rest and is known as *unstable* angina. There is a third type which is even more rare and is called *atypical*, *variant*, or *spastic angina*.

Chronic stable angina

This is, as its name suggests, a very slow-progressing disease which has usually been present for more than six months, by which time the pattern becomes obvious and the diagnosis is made. It is the most common type of angina and usually indicates a long-term buildup of atheroma. It is very predictable and will usually come on with effort or very strong emotion, such as anger or anxiety, both of which can put an excess strain on the heart causing some imbalance to the oxygen supply. It usually fades and disappears with rest and/or glyceryl trinitrate tablets (GTN) or spray. It does not usually last much longer than 10 to 15 minutes.

Unstable angina

This condition is slightly more dangerous than the chronic stable type. It is usually unpredictable and can often occur at rest or during sleep. The symptoms are usually more severe than the usual angina symptoms and the risk of developing a heart attack is a little higher if you have it. The usual symptom may also be accompanied by a panicky sense of impending doom which can be very frightening. In this type of angina the pain occurs repeatedly up to 20 times per day. It usually indicates that a previously stable clot or plaque has detached itself from the heart blood vessel wall or it has become much larger, threatening a heart attack. In an effort to get rid of the blockage, the vessel involved may be contracting and in doing so may temporarily cut off the oxygen supply. Unstable angina requires immediate medical or surgical treatment. Chronic stable angina may become unstable over time.

Atypical angina

This type of angina nearly always occurs when the person is resting or asleep. It is a rare form of angina and is thought to be due to spasm or cramp of the coronary artery which may be a bit like a prolonged twitch in the thin muscle layer of the walls of the arteries. This spasm temporarily restricts the blood flow through the arteries and the oxygen deficit occurs. GTN does not usually relieve this spasm.

Is it possible to have angina without pain?

The simple answer to this question is yes. When an area of the heart is starved of oxygen it is given a medical term – *myo-*

cardial ischaemia. This may or may not produce angina. If it doesn't it is termed *silent ischaemia.* Silent ischaemia is detectable on ECG where it shows the characteristic pattern in the heart tracing (see Fig 9). It can also be seen on more sophisticated tests such as *angiography.* This is where an opaque dye is injected into the coronary arteries and special X-ray photographs are taken of this dye which highlights the shape of the arteries. Ischaemia will show up as a scanty patch of dye as opposed to a full area of dye.

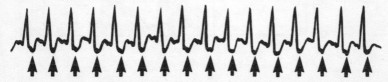

Fig 9: An ECG strip indicating ischaemia (where arrowed)

At some time almost all people with angina will experience some silent myocardial ischaemia. Some people, a small minority, will have repeated attacks which they are totally unaware of. This may be in addition to their painful angina attacks. Silent ischaemia is only dangerous when it is occurring often and unprovoked. Recent research has suggested that silent ischaemia could be the cause of unexplained patterns of breathlessness, fatigue, etc., without pain which occur due to emotional rather than physical triggers.

Does angina have a pattern?

Most people who have angina will eventually be able to predict their own pattern. For some the chances of having an angina attack are greater in the morning up until lunch time and quite a few people will describe having angina whilst showering or getting dressed. For others, their angina occurs in the late evening and/or just before going to bed. The reasons for these patterns are not very clear. People have a different *circadian rhythm* (that is, the natural 24-hour cycles of many bodily processes). However, unlike silent ischaemia, painful ischaemia does not appear to conform to a recognized pattern which is consistent across people. Research evidence shows that there is a true circadian rhythm across people for silent ischaemia. The number of attacks of silent ischaemia are lowest between midnight and 6 a.m., there is a sharp rise between 6 and 8 a.m., and

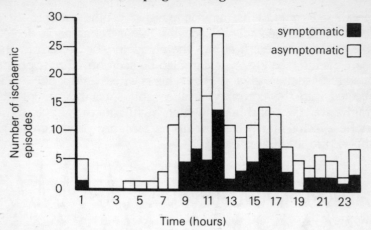

Fig 10: Timing of ischaemic episodes

the greatest number occurs between 8 and 11 a.m. Throughout the day there are frequent attacks, but these steadily decrease up to the lowest point, at midnight.

How does this apply to you?

To summarize briefly, angina is a symptom of coronary disease which varies between people and, depending on the circumstances, within people. It can be provoked by exertion or by emotional/stress factors. Therefore, it is possible to control it by a number of medical methods including tablets, rest or surgery, as discussed in Chapter 2. Your lifestyle may also influence angina and the remaining chapters will teach you how to influence angina by self-control methods. In order to achieve this a healthy and active frame of mind is as important as an active and healthy body. The guidelines in this book are relevant to you and will help you to take care of yourself whether you have had a heart attack or angina or both.

CHAPTER 2

Medical management of angina

Chapter 1 described the narrowing of the coronary arteries and how this gives rise to angina. A doctor initially bases his or her diagnosis of angina entirely on the story a patient relates. The most common symptom is of chest pain but there are many other causes of chest pain from which it must be separated. Further difficulty may arise when angina manifests itself as pain in the jaw, back or arm, or as breathlessness. Physical examination frequently reveals no abnormalities though there are some underlying causes of angina which it is important to recognize. Tests such as the *electrocardiogram* (ECG or 'heart tracing') can be extremely helpful in confirming the diagnosis, and in most cases it is unnecessary to have to go on to more specialized tests such as *coronary angiography* (angiogram or 'dye test'). Once the diagnosis of angina is established, there are many tablets which can help considerably, if not totally control the symptoms of angina. However, under specific circumstances, it is sometimes necessary to consider a *coronary artery bypass graft* operation (CABG or 'bypass') or *angioplasty*.

This chapter considers all these aspects and hopefully will answer many of your questions about the 'technical' side of the management of angina. Your doctor will most likely concentrate on these aspects and there is no doubting their importance. However, once the medical aspects have been fully assessed your doctor will be very happy to know that you are doing something about the other equally important aspects covered in this book.

Initial assessment

The history

Doctors spend a long time getting the story right as it can give

much information as to what is causing chest pain. Not everyone
has the classical 'tight band around the chest' or 'crushing
sensation on the front of the chest' – pains from the oesophagus (the tube leading from the mouth through the chest and
into the stomach) can be very similar. Indeed, patients often
undergo a *barium meal* (X-ray examination of the oesophagus
and stomach) or *gastroscopy* (a look down the oesophagus with
a flexible telescope) when the diagnosis is in doubt. Lung
conditions such as chest infections can also give rise to chest
pains and can often be spotted on a chest X-ray. Muscle strain
and pain from the bones in the spine can also be very similar
in nature, and sometimes when all else is exhausted doctors just
accept that someone has 'chest pain of unknown cause'! There
will be many other questions on smoking habits, alcohol intake,
family history, past illnesses, and exercise which will help build
up a complete picture and highlight any areas where general
advice may be necessary.

The examination

A general physical examination also gives a lot of information on
general well-being, the amount of damage done to the blood
vessels by smoking, the degree of fitness and whether a patient
is overweight. Special attention is paid to the blood pressure and
listening to the heart. *Hypertension* (high blood pressure) is
known to be associated with an increased risk of having a stroke
or a heart attack at some time in the future. By controlling blood
pressure levels, the risk of having a stroke can be markedly
reduced and although there does not appear to be such good
protection against future heart attacks, it is certainly worth
treating this if it is found. An isolated high blood pressure
reading is rarely acted upon as it is recognized that the stress of
seeing a doctor puts it up. Therefore this finding is usually only
an indication for having the blood pressure rechecked on several
separate occasions to get an accurate assessment. By coinci-
dence, if it is found that therapy is required, many of the drugs
used to treat angina such as beta-blockers and calcium antag-
onists are also very good for treating high blood pressure. Lastly,
there are some conditions such as the narrowing of a heart valve
(aortic valve stenosis) which may cause angina, though these
causes are fairly rare.

Blood tests

A blood test may be taken to look for *hyperlipidaemia* (high blood fats) and for a general check on the function of the liver and kidneys. High blood fats, particularly *cholesterol*, are associated with an increased risk of having a heart attack and sometimes very high fat levels run in families. A high cholesterol level may require a particular diet, and sometimes a form of drug therapy in addition. It is now widely accepted that the health of the whole population would be improved by adopting a diet which results in lower cholesterol levels (see Chapter 10).

This first assessment may have been made by the GP (general practitioner). Or the GP may have made a rapid assessment and referred the patient on to a hospital for a specialist opinion from a *cardiologist* (a heart specialist). Either way, following this initial assessment the diagnosis of angina is often clear and some form of therapy may be started. General advice will be given on smoking, weight loss and lifestyle. These topics are covered in more depth than your doctor will have time to cover in Chapters 9 and 10.

Further assessment

The electrocardiograph

The ECG maps out the electrical activity within the heart. The heart is a four-chamber pump which must be carefully controlled and coordinated if it is to function efficiently. The heart has its own 'wiring system' which sends out impulses to the heart muscles. Electrodes placed over the chest wall can pick up these impulses and convert them into a tracing on a strip of paper or on a small television screen. If this wiring goes completely wrong, the heart is unable to beat fast enough or in the correct rhythm. This is when a pacemaker is required to fire off small electrical impulses through the heart to control it correctly. More subtle changes in the electrical pattern can be seen if the heart has suffered a heart attack or is actually having an attack of angina (see Chapter 1). The ECG can therefore show if someone has had a heart attack, though this may not be the case following a very small episode or if the ECG pattern is abnormal for some other reason.

Exercise testing

At rest or during moderate exercise the ECG tracing may be perfectly normal but you know yourself that walking up a particular hill, going out on a cold windy day, or running for the bus may bring on angina. At this time the electrical activity in the heart muscle is also affected and the ECG pattern is changed.

An *exercise tolerance test* (ETT) or 'exercise stress test' is used to see whether exercise under carefully controlled conditions brings on an episode of angina with the characteristic change in ECG pattern. The ECG, heart rate and blood pressure are monitored carefully under the supervision of an experienced doctor and the speed of walking on a treadmill or cycling on an exercise bicycle is gradually increased. The slope of the treadmill may also be changed so that you are walking uphill. The test will be stopped either when angina pain becomes troublesome, or the average amount of exercise for the patient's age is reached, or you get just too tired to continue. The pattern of changes on the ECG can give a lot of information about the underlying blood supply difficulty in the heart. The test may be completed with no apparent problems, which is very reassuring. However, it is always wisest to wait for the full report from the cardiologist, as the ETT may cause ECG changes without producing any symptoms.

Isotope scanning

Another test looking at the blood supply to the heart muscle is the *thallium scan*. A very small and harmless dose of radioactive material is injected into an arm vein and this is carried to the heart where it shows the pattern of blood flow through the heart on a piece of equipment called a gamma camera placed over the front of the chest. An exercise test may be performed at the same time, or a drug may be injected into the arm vein which speeds up the heart and makes it work harder. This can show up any areas of the heart with a reduced blood supply and in effect is a way of exercising the heart without putting the patient on the treadmill. As a picture of the blood flow through the heart is produced by the gamma camera, this can give extra useful information. There are other forms of isotope heart scans which are used to measure how well the heart is working as a pump, though these are not routinely used when investigating coronary heart disease.

These tests can give useful information about the blood flow through the coronary arteries. However, most patients with angina can be managed perfectly well without resorting to these tests. They are usually only undertaken when extra information is required. This may be when the diagnosis is not clear or if the angina is particularly severe and not being very well controlled by drug therapy. Another situation when extra tests are performed is following a heart attack when it is necessary to find out whether a patient might benefit from coronary artery surgery.

Coronary angiography

The 'gold standard' test to find out what is happening inside the coronary arteries is the angiogram. All the above tests can be performed with you as an outpatient but it is usual to spend a short spell of 24 or 48 hours in hospital for an angiogram. This test is performed in a room like an operating theatre. A catheter (a small plastic tube) is placed into an artery in an arm or groin after the skin has been numbed with a local anaesthetic injection. It is then fed back up the main artery of the body to the heart. The catheter is followed on its course back to the heart on an X-ray machine which can give a continuous picture on a television screen. When the tube gets near the heart it can be carefully placed within each coronary artery in turn and dye injected into it. This picture of the arteries is recorded on film.

The resulting picture of the coronary arteries can show exactly where a narrowing or blockage occurs. Under certain circumstances an operation may be indicated to open up these narrow arteries or to bypass the narrowed segment. This will be dealt with in greater detail towards the end of this chapter. Undergoing this test can be frightening as the doctors and nurses wear gowns and masks and the machinery used is large and sometimes noisy. Don't be afraid to ask questions of your doctors before the angiogram as this is difficult to do during the test and you may be given a drug to make you feel more relaxed. Following the test you will be asked to lie still to reduce any possibility of bleeding from the puncture site in the artery. This is another chance to ask questions of the medical staff though remember that little information may be available until the film can be examined in greater detail. Due to the anxiety of a hospital admission you may not remember all that is told you by the staff so at the next hospital visit don't be afraid to take your husband or wife or a friend with you and ask for full explanations, in writing if necessary, and diagrams if you are unsure of what is being said.

All these tests are done regularly on many hundreds of patients in any large hospital and very few problems occur. However, these tests may bring on an attack of angina though this should be quickly relieved by treatment from the medical staff. If you feel unwell with chest pains or breathlessness following any of these tests, do inform the medical staff.

Drug treatment

The oldest treatment of angina, *glyceryl trinitrate* (GTN) has been used for many years and remains a very useful drug. However, many different drugs have now been developed which can be helpful in angina. Indeed, new drugs continue to be developed and you may even be asked to help in studies of the effectiveness of new drugs in some hospitals. No one drug will suit or work for everyone and sometimes several may have to be tried before the best is found for an individual. Combinations of different types of drugs may be very effective when used together and it is not unusual to require two or more different drugs to fully control angina symptoms.

Nitrates

GTN tablets placed under the tongue have effectively treated angina attacks for many years. They act by dilating the veins which return blood to the heart, thereby reducing the workload on the heart. GTN is derived from the explosive TNT and the only common side-effect is the production of headaches (not explosive in nature!). Very occasionally, they may cause a faint. They rapidly relieve an attack of angina within minutes though some people may need 2 or 3 tablets for a full effect – if it is not effective then a doctor should be consulted. They can also be used to prevent attacks of angina coming on. If there is a particular activity which is known to bring on angina, then GTN, taken immediately prior to that activity, can allow it to be pain-free. The tablets lose their activity after several months and become ineffective beyond the expiry date on the bottle. Partly because of this problem, but also because it is more convenient and may be more rapidly effective, GTN is often delivered in

Table 1 Drug therapy for angina

Group	Generic Name	Proprietary Names	Disadvantages of Possible Side Effects
Nitrates	Isosorbide mononitrate	Elantan, Indus, Ismo	Headaches when first starting treatment
	Isosorbide dinitrate	Cedocard, Isordil, Sorbitrate	
Beta-blockers	Propranolol Antenolol Metoprolol Pindolol Nodolol Oxprenolol	Inderal Tenormin Betaloc, Lopressor Betadren, Visken Corgard Trasicor	Not suitable for asthma sufferers and people with heart failure or poor circulation. May produce *wheeze*, cold extremities, nightmares, slow heart rate, dizziness, fatigue, difficulties with sexual function
Calcium antagonists	Nifedipine Diltiazam Verapamil	Adalat Tildiem Cordilox, Securon	May not be suitable for people with other heart conditions. May produce flushing of the skin, ankle swelling, palpitations, dizziness. Rarely worsens angina.

*N.B. This table is *not* meant to be comprehensive.

spray form. A small 'squirter' aerosol delivers two puffs under the tongue where it is rapidly absorbed into the circulation. There is no benefit from trying to 'hold off' using GTN – it should be used whenever angina comes on. The body does not become 'used to' repeated doses.

Delivered under the tongue, as opposed to swallowed, GTN is effective because it goes directly into the bloodstream and avoids being destroyed in the stomach and liver. Tablet forms of nitrates have been developed which resist this destruction and can reduce the frequency of angina episodes when taken regularly by mouth. These may also produce headaches when first started though again these usually wear off completely after 2–3 weeks. This group of drugs is still called 'nitrates' and the formal scientific name (generic name) for the most commonly used nitrate taken by mouth is **isosorbide mononitrate**. Pharmaceutical companies manufacture tablets in different ways causing the rate of absorption from the stomach to vary and so some forms may be more rapidly acting while others may be longer lasting. Tablets may need to be taken once or up to three times a day, depending on these factors. Each pharmaceutical company will call its own tablet by a different name (proprietary name) so that the differences will be clear to the prescribing doctor and pharmacist. However, some companies make the same drug and call it by a different name – confusing, isn't it! The final point about nitrate tablets is that the timing of taking them can be important to obtain the maximum benefit and to avoid a reduced effect in some situations – discuss with your doctor the most efficient use for your own lifestyle and angina.

Nitrates are also available in the form of a cream kept against the skin under a type of adhesive plaster or against the gums in a pastille. With these GTN patches the drug is absorbed through the skin or gums and can be very effective in some people. However, many people find they become less effective with time and may cause local irritation. They are tending to become less popular for these reasons though they remain very satisfactory for some people.

Beta-blockers (β-blockers)

These drugs have revolutionized the therapy of angina and hypertension. They take this name from their ability to block a specific mechanism which activates cells, in particular the muscle cells found in the heart and blood vessels. They slow the heart down and reduce the workload put on the heart. They are very effective at reducing the frequency of angina episodes and allowing a greater amount of exertion before angina comes on. Initially they had to be taken three or four times a day but new beta-blockers have been developed and older ones reformulated by the pharmaceutical companies, so that most can be taken once or twice a day for 24-hour protection.

Newer drugs tend to have fewer side-effects but they are nearly always unsuitable for asthma sufferers and sometimes for people with chronic chest disorders due to smoking. A common side-effect is cold hands and feet. This is usually mild and not troublesome, but if there is a degree of blockage of the arteries in the legs then again these drugs may not be suitable. Likewise, patients taking diuretics (water tablets) for heart failure may be advised to avoid these drugs. Table 1 shows other side-effects which may occur, though in general these drugs are extremely well tolerated by most patients. It may not be realized that the onset of nightmares has been caused by taking a new drug therapy but they can be quite frightening and it is not unknown for them to induce angina! Slowing of the heart rate is to be expected and is not usually a problem, though on occasions when the heart rate normally speeds up with exertion or on standing up quickly, the slow heart rate can cause a reduced energy level for exercise or a drop in blood pressure causing dizziness. The onset of sexual difficulties, particularly maintaining an erection, may also be associated with beta-blockers. Stress in general and worry over angina occurring during sexual intercourse can also affect sexual performance. Try not to be shy in discussing these aspects with your medical advisers. Problems may indeed respond to a change in drug therapy though help from a counsellor is sometimes required. Chapter 8 discusses some of these points in further detail.

There are so many beta-blockers available that only some of the more commonly used ones are included in the table. Which one is used will depend on your doctor's knowledge of your health and what is known about the effects of the drug.

Calcium antagonists

These are relatively new drugs which, like beta-blockers, affect the excitability of muscle cells within the heart and blood vessels, but do so by a different mechanism. Also like beta-blockers they are used for both angina and hypertension. The three main types of calcium antagonist have definite differences which make some more suitable than others for specific patients. The first to be used widely for angina was **nifedipine,** which is particularly effective at reducing spontaneous spasm of the coronary arteries, and, therefore, angina occurring at rest or during sleep. It is also very effective in hypertension. There was some initial worry over reports that it could make angina worse, though experience has shown this to be a fairly unusual problem. Although nifedipine is effective is also tends to be the drug most likely to induce flushing with a hot sensation in the skin which may become red. This occurs 30 minutes to one hour after taking the drug and can last for a few hours. It is sometimes associated with palpitations, dizziness or feeling faint. Another common problem is the development of ankle swelling. Together these may occur in 20–30 per cent of patients and will mean the drug should be discontinued unless the benefit is of greater value to the patient than the discomfort caused by these side-effects. The oldest of these drugs is **verapamil** and it does not tend to be associated with these problems. However, the original use of verapamil was to control abnormal heart rhythms and it has only recently become widely used for angina and hypertension. It is usually avoided in patients with heart failure and is not usually used together with beta-blockers. **Diltiazam** possibly has the fewest side-effects and is quite specific for treating angina, though currently it has the disadvantage that it must be taken three times a day.

Other drugs

Aspirin used as a painkiller is one of the oldest pharmaceutical drugs in existence. Research has shown that it also has profound effects on the function of those factors in the bloodstream and the walls of blood vessels which play a part in blood clotting. These factors can induce angina in some patients and this can be improved by taking a small daily dose of aspirin. Aspirin is often recommended routinely following coronary artery bypass surgery or angioplasty because of these properties. There is a fashion in the USA for everyone to start taking aspirin when they reach 'middle age'. This is in the belief that reducing the activity of the blood clotting factors may prevent a clot in a coronary artery and thus prevent a heart attack. While there is some evidence that this is so in people who already have suffered a heart attack, the evidence is less convincing for the average 'man or woman in the street'. The main problem with regular aspirin ingestion is that it can cause or worsen indigestion and duodenal or gastric ulcers. An enteric coated form (sugar coated) has been developed to minimize this problem. Aspirin may interact with other drugs and you should always check with your doctor before starting on regular medication even if bought without prescription. Fish oil and evening primrose oil capsules have a similar theoretical effect to aspirin on the clotting factors but there is no firm proof to date that they are useful.

The aim of drug therapy is to obtain the maximum amount of relief from angina using the minimum number of drugs while avoiding significant side-effects. The most common starting point is to use a GTN spray when required and this is sufficient for many. However, when everday life is being interrupted by angina, one of the above drugs will usually be prescribed. It sometimes takes a change of drug on one or two occasions to find one that suits and it may be necessary to use a combination of two or even three of these agents. When large amounts of medication are required it is often an indication for going on to the exercise test and/or thallium scan, and/or an angiogram to see whether an operation is indicated.

Surgical treatment

Angioplasty

In the usual sense this is not an operation as the procedure is carried out during an angiogram, though a cardiac surgeon is always available in case it is necessary to proceed to a full operation (this is a rare occurrence). If a very localized narrowing of a coronary artery is seen on the arteriogram picture an angioplasty may be performed at that time or arranged for a later date. During the angiogram procedure a catheter with a 'balloon' attachment is passed into the coronary artery. This is then passed carefully over a guide wire and past the narrowed segment of the coronary artery.

When the balloon is at the narrow part of the artery it is

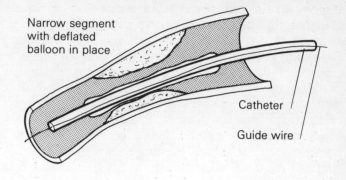

Narrow segment
with deflated
balloon in place

Catheter

Guide wire

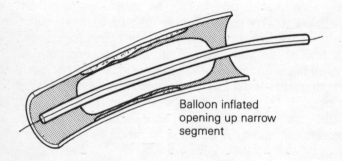

Balloon inflated
opening up narrow
segment

Fig 11: Angioplasty

carefully inflated. This compresses the material which is narrowing the artery up against the artery wall and leaves a clear passage for blood to flow through. The compressed material is made of fatty substances, white blood cells and fibrous tissue and causes no problem once flattened against the artery wall. It is possible that some of it is carried away by 'scavenger cells' in the blood stream. The simple precaution of staying in hospital for two or three days is necessary to ensure that no problems arise. Drugs such as aspirin and others which help with blood flow may be recommended following an angioplasty and it may be necessary to check the results with a repeat angiogram at a later date. This treatment is an important advance in heart surgery. It is not a major procedure and it can be dramatically successful in some cases. However, it is only appropriate for a minority of patients and is not always successful in relieving angina. Also the angina may return, requiring a repeat angio-plasty or coronary artery bypass grafting.

Coronary artery bypass grafting (CABG)

As this is a major heart operation it is not to be taken lightly! However, patients in two situations can be greatly helped by CABG. Firstly, it can have a dramatic effect in those whose lives are seriously disrupted by angina, when, despite drug therapy, a normal everyday life has become impossible. Secondly, certain other patients have a narrowing of a particularly important coronary artery or combination of coronary arteries. Bypassing these blockages can not only relieve angina but also reduce the chances of a heart attack happening in the future. Despite the major benefits, careful consideration has to be given to each case before going ahead as it involves a general anaesthetic, opening the chest and operating on the heart surface where the coronary arteries run. While it is now a relatively safe procedure, there is always the possibility of complications, and following the operation a period of two to three months' recovery must be expected before full activity is restored.

The principle is to divert the blood flow around a narrow segment of coronary artery so that blood can be delivered to the

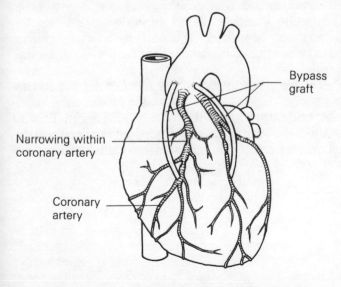

Bypass graft

Narrowing within coronary artery

Coronary artery

Fig 12: Bypass grafting

heart muscle beyond and so relieve the angina. The material used for the bypass is a piece of vein from your own leg. This is because if synthetic materials are used they quickly become blocked by blood clots. Your leg can manage perfectly well without the small piece of vein which is removed. Frequently, patients remember very little of the first few days following a CABG as some time is usually spent under sedation in the Intensive Care or Therapy Unit (ICU or ITU) to keep a close watch on the situation.

Understandably there will be generalized weakness and a lot of soreness in the chest wall where the stitches are. Some of the stitches holding the breastbone together are wire and are not removed. This discomfort may take several weeks or sometimes months to settle down. There may also be some discomfort and swelling in the leg where the vein was taken from (this is often helped by a support stocking). After several weeks a full return to previous activities and, if advised, increased activity can be expected.

It if obviously important to try to prevent the graft from clotting up once all this trouble has been gone to! Particular attention will be paid to not smoking and keeping the blood cholesterol levels down. It cannot be emphasized too much how important stopping smoking is in this process. Drugs, some previously discussed, will be prescribed to reduce the clotting tendency of the blood and in some situations blood thinning tablets, usually **warfarin,** may be prescribed. The dose of warfarin tablets would need to be controlled by regular blood tests, usually at the hospital.

Despite all these considerations, the relief of angina in the majority of patients makes CABG a valuable procedure. Unfortunately, the underfunding of the health services in Britain means that this relatively expensive procedure is not as widely available as desired and a waiting list is inevitable at this time.

How to get the best out of your doctor

● Always ask for explanations of anything you do not understand. If necessary, take a list of questions with you when you see the doctor. Don't be afraid to ask someone to go with you.

● Ask your doctor to write information down for you or draw diagrams if it is at all complicated.

● You may find diagrams and words used in this chapter are used by your doctor, but you would like an explanation of how it applies to you. Show the doctor the relevant page, or write it down on a sheet with your list of questions, so the doctor can discuss it with you.

● Describe to your doctor any worries you have about your condition or its treatment, as there is often a simple explanation which can be very reassuring.

● Do your best to take your medication as directed – if you have difficulties then ask for a different or simpler drug regimen if possible.

● Appreciate that the doctor is only part of a team looking after you – physiotherapist, dietitian, nurses all play their part. The most important member of the team is you, the patient, with a realization that how you live your life may be the most important factor in deciding how well you remain in the future.

CHAPTER 3

Stress:
what does it mean to you?

Everyone knows what stress is. Stress is . . .

- overwork, boredom, dissatisfaction, conflict
- butterflies, aches and strains
- crises, disasters, panic.

But if you pin people down, they will tell you some puzzling, paradoxical, things about stress:

- It is bad for you sometimes, but some people thrive on it.
- Not everyone feels stressed by the same situation: some people like crowds and head for the busiest part of the room at parties, others prefer to be on their own or with a few good friends.
- You can feel stressed by one situation today, like arranging a hospital appointment, but not be bothered about it next time.
- Some people become ill with stress. They have rashes, headaches, panic attacks and chest pains, while others seem to remain fairly healthy.

So although stress is a common word, we need to tease out these paradoxes which hold the clue to how you can understand *your* stress response and learn to manage your stress – to unlock your own potential to win.

Part of the paradox can be unravelled by looking at some different models of stress or ways of thinking about stress which you may be using.

A model is only useful if it helps us explain how you react in as many situations as possible. This allows you to *predict* and *decide* if you want to *control* how you will respond in future.

Stress is . . . how you think, feel and behave

Think back to the last time you had a real fright; you nearly crashed the car, got an outsized bill, heard bad news about a relative or your work. How did you feel? What thoughts went through your mind? What action did you take? Answers to these questions will help you to describe your typical *acute* or immediate response to stress.

You may be aware of a whole range of physical effects in your body; tension in your muscles of your face, neck, arms, chest, stomach and legs. You may notice your mouth drying up, your heartbeat and breathing quickening, your face flushing or going pale, your stomach churning, your bowel and bladder feeling full. Your sight and hearing may seem very sharp. Your thoughts may race, time seeming to stretch, then immediately afterwards events seem to have taken place in a flash. Your behaviour may include speaking loudly, making hurried movements, physically bracing yourself into a self-protective or aggressive stance.

In a matter of hours, if you try to sustain this level of response, you will tire. Your bodily responses will include aches and fatigue, nausea and poor appetite, your senses will seem less sharp. You may also get angina. Your thoughts will be less clear, and you may even think irrationally, taking events out of context and blowing them out of all proportion. Your behaviour will probably be more clumsy, your actions less strong and decisive.

In the much longer term, with stressful events adding up over a period of years, people become more prone to stress-related disorders. Each person inherits tendencies to develop particular disorders, but these only emerge when the person is put under extensive and intensive stress. No single disorder can be produced solely by stress, each depends to an extent on what is inherited, and what environmental hazards (such as heavy lifting jobs for back pain, airborne pollutants for breathing disorders such as asthma or bronchitis) you are exposed to.

Also, in a person who has developed the disorder, periods of severe symptoms may coincide with stressful periods in their life. For example, a person who is prone to headache pain may only get headaches at the end of a working week, and seldom during holidays or a weekend. Whether you develop a habit of being stressed depends on the amount of demands or *stressful events* in your life.[1]

Stress is . . . the demands put on you

Air crashes, motorway pile-ups, hurricanes, wars and other major disasters seem pretty strong bets as events that would stress anyone. There is plenty of evidence that people show very strong reactions of shock, emotional distress, and disturbance of their ability to do everyday tasks for days and sometimes months afterwards, and their health suffers.[2] There is a higher rate of heart attacks in communities exposed to sudden disaster.

At a more everyday level, we know that some commoner events such as the death of a close relative, divorce, and bankruptcy are distressing to most people. Research on naval recruits also showed that mainly positive events are also stressful; going on vacation can be as stressful as getting caught for a traffic offence. This is because stress occurs when a *demand* is made on the person and he or she believes they may be unable to meet the challenge and may suffer unpleasant consequences. So, while planning a holiday, you may be worried about getting ill while abroad or the possible hidden costs which will take you over your budget.

Some events are given much the same rating by groups of people taken on average. That is, if you asked a group of car assemblers at a local factory and a group of managers at the same plant, they might all rate bankruptcy, pregnancy in the family and holidays in the same order from worst to best.

But this glosses over the impact that one event such as pregnancy might have for your family. It could be a wonderful gift long sought after, or an unwanted emotional and financial burden.

Similarly, redundancy can be a blessing with a large pay cheque to be used to start up a new business, or a frustrating end to a promising career. This is true even for really devastating events like a heart attack, which can have some inescapably distressing effects. But these effects can be partly remedied by small positive gains such as the perhaps unexpected experience of real warmth and support from the family. And surprisingly, this fact goes for people who have survived really large-scale disasters such as the Bradford City Football Club fire, the Zeebrugge ferry disaster, the Piper Alpha oil platform disaster, the Lockerbie and M1 air disasters, and the experience of hijack victims in the Middle East. Not everyone who suffers a major disaster is lastingly scarred by it. Those who recover and put the experience behind them seem to be those who are able to find some positive aspects of the event, and to feel they have learnt something useful about themselves.

One survivor of a motorway pile-up who was badly burned and treated at the Birmingham Accident Hospital said to me: 'OK, I'm physically scarred. I have mottled skin on my neck and hands, and I don't look so handsome now, I guess! But I got out of the car, and I'm still not sure how, when I saw it catch fire. I knew only I could save myself, and I did it. That feels good. And I'm much closer to my wife now, we really appreciate the time we have together now, and that has to be good.'

Freda had a heart attack at 55 years old. She was a successful businesswoman, with her own secretarial agency, and two grown-up children by her first husband. She developed severe angina after her heart attack, and was advised to sell her business. She felt it was too soon to retire fully. But on the other hand, she looks back two years later with some relief, since she felt worried before the heart attack that she had not allowed herself to develop new personal relationships. She is now remarried and has a smaller agency which she feels keeps her mind ticking over, but allows her more time for her family.

So, stress is *not* simply a direct result of the amount of demand put on a person. Rather, each person responds differently to the same events, and every event has both distressing and positive effects depending upon *how* the person assesses the likely impact of the event on their unique personal circumstances.[3]

Is all stress harmful?

We already know that there is no simple relationship between the disastrousness of an event and the amount of stress a person feels. This is because we all differ in how we feel that event will affect us. It is also true that we have our own capacity for coping with stress. If there is little or no demand on us, we get bored, or 'rust out'. But with a higher level of demand, or 'push' from our work and leisure commitments, we thrive. Many studies of workers in production plants, in the armed forces and the professions such as medicine and nursing, show that people welcome and work better if 'stretched' to meet demands. But each person has a different point at which they can do no more. Further demand, far from pushing up production, produces much lower output. That is, people go over their optimum, and into 'burn out'.[4] (See Fig 13.)

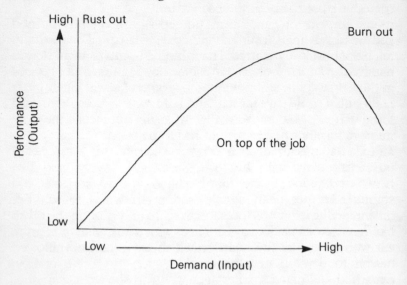

Fig 13: Relationship between demands, performance and stress:
the Human Response Curve

For people with angina, the diagnosis of a serious and permanent heart condition can be devastating. For some, it is the first stage in a vicious cycle of failure.

John was a skilled engineering worker before he began to get chest pains, leading to a referral to the company doctor and eventually to a diagnosis of angina. He was able to remain at work, but found his symptoms of tiredness and breathlessness affected his work. He tried to redouble his efforts, and began to follow his own fitness programme to build up his strength. He noticed little improvement, and began to feel guilty and angry with himself for not acting earlier to prevent his heart problem. He became anxious, he felt panicky every time he got chest symptoms. The symptoms got worse when he was tense, which made him worry about going to work. He began to have problems sleeping, which added to his problem of fatigue in the daytime, and made it virtually impossible for him to concentrate at work. He went into hospital for a diagnosis of acute chest pain which he thought was a heart attack. It turned out to be an ischaemic attack (angina pain) but his boss took the opportunity to make him redundant. He was fearful of activity provoking angina so he took less exercise. He became physically deconditioned. That is, the same exercise took more energy, putting more demand on his heart. This led to a shortage of blood getting to the heart, causing angina. He became lethargic and felt helpless. He felt his life was broken by his illness, and his life revolved around his symptoms. He became a drain on his family and less and less confident in his role as a father and husband. He felt that now that he was redundant he was worthless. As a lover, his fear of angina and of having a heart attack during sexual intercourse made him impotent. He was left feeling a total failure, and found little reason for living.

Everyone reacts differently to the stress of the diagnosis of heart disease. But not everyone reacts in such a pessimistic and self-fulfilling way. Those that cope are those who manage not to take the cause of their disease as solely their fault. But they *do* feel responsible for how they react and manage their illness. It can be regarded as a crisis. Or it can be a challenge, the chance of change, sometimes for the better, as Freda discovered (see page 51).

Returning to the paradoxes described at the beginning of the chapter, the models of stress as either a direct result of certain types of unpleasant events, or a set of predictable physical, thinking, emotional and behavioural responses, must be re-examined. Any model must account for the way the *individual* interprets an event. Research on the physical response of victims of fatal car crashes shows that at autopsy, there was evidence of an adrenal response (physical stress) in those who had some prior warning of the crash, if only seconds. The bodies of people killed instantly showed no signs of stress. This proves that it takes a person's interpretation of an event to activate physical responses (known as the 'fight or flight' response). Further, since the bodily symptoms of tension are often a cue to action, and bodily responses affect behaviour (such as the coordination of arm and body movements), a model which suggests that these responses interact may give a person some cues for change as in Fig 14:[5,6]

For example, the event or trigger could be driving your car into a near collision with a tree because of ice on the road. Your responses may seem to be automatic, almost so fast you can't think, although some thought *is* necessary or you wouldn't recognize danger and act to save yourself. Your thoughts trigger

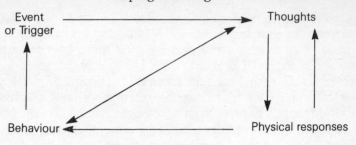

Fig 14: Stress model

both physical responses of steering the car, braking and releasing your brake, and protecting yourself from impact by bracing yourself. Your physical state (muscle tension, fingers gripping the wheel, heart racing) are signals to you of your stress. This may be interpreted as a signal you are out of control, producing panic thoughts such as 'Help, I'm unable to control the wheel, my arms are rigid, I'll crash.' Alternatively, you could interpret these bodily and behaviour reactions as natural self-defence and be reassured, thinking 'It's okay, I'm alert and able to see the danger, I'll make it.'

This model of how stressful events and stress responses interact will be explored in Chapters 5 and 7. But as it stands, it is missing an important ingredient. Your thoughts are crucial to how you respond to stress and this depends on your past history of tackling similar events. This past history helps to form your *personality* or preferred *coping style*.

Stress is . . . your personality

We can all think of people we know in our families and at work who seem to attract stress. These stress-prone people seem to thrive on competition, are often the first to take on new tasks, often before finishing another one. They may also be short-tempered or rather highly strung people. It is unlikely all these characteristics exist in one person, but all are typical of people who attract stress to themselves. They will also influence how a new stressful event is understood and acted upon. These individual differences are generally well-established in your personality but once you understand them, you have the choice of making changes which may make you less stress-prone. These personal coping styles are examined in Chapter 5.

Putting it all together

1. Stress affects everyone, but each person reacts differently. A stressful event for one person is not necessarily a stressful event for someone else, and may not be stressful to that person on other occasions.

2. Stress is good in moderation, but too many stressful events at once can lead to a decline in productivity and well-being.

3. Stress responses follow predictable *general* patterns in the short term, particularly the physical 'fight or flight' response.

4. But in the longer term, due to each person's past history of success or failure in learning to cope with stress as well as the availability of buffers to stress, a person's response to stress may lead to healthy action or less healthy physical and emotional deterioration.

CHAPTER 4

Angina and stressful events

Stress is a result of events which put demands upon people. But the same event can be interpreted in different ways. For example, going into hospital can be a threat to someone who thinks they have a burst appendix, and a joy to another who is due to have a baby. The meaning of the event determines whether the event is seen to be a threat or a wonderful opportunity. This chapter examines the meaning of stressful events and how to cope with them.

Everyone faces demands of many kinds daily. These minor events include such events as:

- bad weather
- noise
- planning and preparing meals
- travel
- traffic jams
- conflict with a partner or work colleague
- missing buses, being late for appointments
- equipment breaking down
- having a heavy cold.

Not all of these 'hassles' are necessarily bad, such as travel, but nevertheless, demand is put on the person to take decisions or to do things in a short space of time. The more minor hassles a person has in a day, the more stress is experienced as emotional strain and physical arousal, leading eventually to exhaustion.

The two keys to whether a person feels stressed by minor hassles are firstly, if the events all pile upon each other or come on top of a more important life crisis, such as a bereavement, and secondly, how the person interprets their likely ability to cope with it.

Table 2 Stressful life events

Events – some examples	Stress rating
Death of a spouse/partner Divorce or separation Death of a close family member Major injury or illness Loss of a job Going to prison	high
Marital reconciliation Retirement Injury or ill-health of a family member Pregnancy Gain of a new family member Death of a close friend	moderately high
Large mortgage Foreclosure of a loan Change in work responsibilities Outstanding personal achievement Conflict with the boss	moderate
Change in work hours Moving house Having a small loan Going on holiday Christmas	low

(Based on Holmes and Rahe, 1967[1])

Before turning to *how* to cope with hassles and life crises, it is helpful to learn more about the types of events which cause stress. Identifying the causes of stress is the first step in predicting future stress and in triggering new ways of coping.

Recent experience of life crises, or 'life events' as researchers have called major events which cause change and increase demands upon people, is associated with more feelings of stress. In a major transport disaster, when a person may be badly injured and face their own death and the loss of fellow travellers including perhaps their family, they will experience a number of life crises all at once. This causes maximum demand on all emotional, physical and financial reserves. But life crises can be equally stressful if they occur one on top of the other over a period of time, with little chance to recover in between or to anticipate and plan for the next crisis. Bankruptcy, for example, can cause a series of losses: of work, money, goods, social standing and self-esteem. The bankrupt may feel others have taken over, causing sudden new changes such as the mortgage company repossessing the house.

A greater degree of stress occurs when a large number of crises occur together. Table 2 shows some life events which have been banded together in groups according to whether samples of people in many different walks of life believe they are more or less stressful?[2]

In general, the more of the high-ranked life events experienced by a person in a short space of time, the more stress they experience and the more likely they are to develop serious stress-related illnesses such as heart disease and ulcers. But it is also true that stress is not inevitable, since it depends on how the person believes the event will affect them and how well they are able to ward off any threatening effects.[3,4]

Think for yourself of the following events and what they mean to you:

1. One or more real stressful events which have happened to you in the last year. This might include having a heart attack, losing your job or moving house, or having a brush with the law.
2. One or more major events which occurred in the last year which did not cause stress to you. This might include being made redundant with a large payoff, going on a long holiday, winning a prize or taking up a new hobby.
3. Two or three events or hassles which irritate you, your 'pet

hate'.[5] This might be dogs fouling the pavement near where you live, traffic jams, or party political broadcasts.

4. Two or three everyday events you encounter which do not cause stress to you but might stress others, such as taking up an important role on a committee, public speaking or being called for jury service.

Try to get a list of at least two events for each category listed on the left hand side of Table 3.

Table 3 Reaction to stressful events

Event	What I feel about it	Why I feel this way about these events
1. Major stressful event: 1. 2.		
Example: Had heart attack.	Fear, frustration.	Lack of control. Fear for my life.
2. Major events/ not stressful: 1. 2.		
Example: Changing job.	Excitement and challenge.	In control, believe I can do it.
3. Everyday hassle: 1. 2. 3.		
Example: Dog fouled the pavement.	Angry and frustrated.	I can't stop them.
4. Everyday event/ not stressful: 1. 2. 3.		
Example: Voted in to chair of Committee.	Proud.	I can do it, in control, will be good at it, successful.

Under the section on the right 'What I feel about this event', write down your *emotional reaction* to the event. E.g: opposite the everyday hassle of party political broadcasts you might write 'irritated'. Try to write your feelings in one or two words for each example.

Write down one or more reasons for your emotional reaction to each event. You can simply put words such as 'lack of control', 'fear of failure and embarrassment', 'fear of pain', or 'pretty sure of success' by each example.

The importance of this exercise is to see that events are not stressful in themselves, but can cause stress if the event is a real *threat* to our values, our well-being, health, livelihood and relationships, and either:

1. predictable and unavoidable, or
2. unpredictable and unavoidable, or
3. predictable but controllable with planning or effort during and after the event.

The next section looks at the causes of the stressfulness of events at work and in home and leisure time in more detail, in order to identify some of the key elements of what makes events stressful for each person and what can be done to make changes.

Coping with stressful events

Managing predictable and unavoidable events

- Imagine being told at work your boss has to lose half his staff and you are on the redundancy list.
- Imagine your family doctor asks to see you about your partner's health. She explains your partner is expected to live no more than 6 months.
- Imagine the local council has decided to put a road through your garden and is offering you compensation.
- Imagine your partner has inherited a large sum of money from a distant relative.

All of these events are sudden and at least partially unpredictable. Depending upon your circumstances, you might interpret redundancy as welcome or unwelcome, the death of your partner as a catastrophic shock for a shortened happy life or a relief from

years of suffering. Similarly, forcible house purchase and inherit-
ance can be burdens or blessings. While there are obvious
practical actions that must be taken depending upon the exact
circumstances, some general rules will apply to most predictable
and unavoidable events:

1. Identify all aspects of the event which cause you to feel threatened

E.g. the threat of redundancy:

- Will it really happen, and when?
- What alternatives do I have?
- What costs will it bring to me personally?
- Are there any benefits for me now, and in the longer term?
- Should I feel a failure or are other circumstances beyond my control to blame?

In practice, most of the answers can be obtained by talking to
people in charge of the situation, or others who have been in
your position before. These are the practical actions most people
will carry out when faced with a real-life predictable threat.
However, they often overlook the personal, emotional and
physical health impact of the event. Dealing with these feelings
and bolstering your healthy coping reactions are especially
important.

2. Identify the personal impact of the event

- Do you feel responsible for the event?
- Do you feel responsible for how the event affects you?
- Do you feel in control of how you will respond?
- How do you feel about other people's reactions?
- Do you anticipate success or failure?

3. Identify what you can do to manage your feelings about the event

- Let feelings out, both on your own and with supportive people.
- Think through the problem and what can be learned from it.
- Talk with people who can support you through the problem, or take some of this and other burdens away.
- Give yourself 'time out' at regular intervals from the problem so you have time for emotional repair.

4. Identify what you can do to bolster your health and well-being during this stressful time

- Make sure you stick to a healthy daily lifestyle of balanced food, exercise, relaxation, and avoid excessive alcohol and smoking.

- Avoid taking on other heavy demands during this time.
- Delegate or say no to additional daily hassles, keeping these to a minimum.
- Allow yourself real breaks away from the problem. For example, try to mix with some friends who do not know about it or who can be trusted to let you leave the problem behind for a short time.

An example of how a person with angina dealt with the threat of major heart surgery is given by the case of Barbara:

At 49 years old, Barbara had had angina for two years. Her symptoms were steadily getting more severe until she was unable to walk up more than ten stairs without becoming breathless and having strong chest pains.

Her physician referred her to the heart surgeon who examined her coronary arteries during a cardiac catheterization procedure. She was found to have one artery more than 50 per cent blocked and one artery 80 per cent blocked. The surgeon advised her to have coronary bypass surgery, so she was put on a 6-month waiting list.

Barbara felt relieved that some treatment was available, but angry that she had to wait, and also very fearful about the pain and risk of the operation as well as the disruption to her work and family plans. However, she talked it over with her physician, and her husband and the chief coronary surgery nurse. She asked to talk to patients who had been through the operation and was introduced to the 'Mended Hearts' post-bypass support group run by the hospital social worker. She talked to her family doctor about ways of keeping healthy and he agreed to give her monthly check-ups if she attended the health promotion class run in his practice.

She coped well until an unrelated crisis occurred. Her husband's small business crashed. She knew she had coped reasonably well when his business had been in trouble before, but this seemed to be too much to cope with on top of her own troubles. Her husband blamed some of his business failure on the worry and expense of his wife's illness. She realized they would both suffer if she let her health problems become an excuse for their marital and financial problems. After discussion with her husband they both agreed to get financial advice, and if their marriage did not improve when the financial worries were under control, to seek marriage guidance counselling. In the meantime, they decided to take a short break with old friends of theirs to give themselves a little breathing space.

So, even inevitable, predictable and unavoidable crises can be met either as an overwhelming catastrophe, or as a series of problems which can be tackled individually and systematically. This approach emphasizes that successful outcomes may not be achievable even with the best efforts, but that during the time when the crisis is anticipated, attempting to identify what is achievable and working towards those goals can reintroduce a sense of personal control.

Managing unpredictable and unavoidable events

- Imagine shovelling snow and getting a sudden, crushing chest pain. Next thing you know you are in an Intensive Care Unit in hospital.
- Imagine being woken up by the smell of burning coming from downstairs, your house is on fire and your children are asleep in the third floor attic bedroom with no fire escape.
- Imagine going into work to find a television crew in your office and a presentation ceremony organized by your boss who has selected you as the best worker of the year.
- Imagine winning the local lottery first prize of five thousand pounds.

Each situation you have imagined may fill you with feelings of fear, panic, and confusion. The crises which involve threats to your life or to your relatives' lives will almost always involve real emotional pain. The crises with the promise of success and personal gain may still fill you with dread as well as pleasure, since public honour and attention is not always welcomed. How you react again depends upon what that event means to you. And again, there are helpful and unhelpful methods of coping.

Research on how people cope with major disasters shows that those who come out of it best, with fewest emotional problems, are those who can talk about the problems and their feelings within hours of the event. But talking is not enough, it is also necessary to identify what practical problems must be overcome and at the same time to identify what emotions are aroused and how these can be understood and channelled into a sense of personal control and purpose.

Returning to an event which could happen to many readers of this book, that of having a heart attack and waking up in hospital.

1. Identify those aspects of the event which threaten you

● How badly affected are you?
● What danger are you in?
● What can be done to minimize your danger?
● What risks do you take of trying to help yourself?

2. Identify the personal impact of the event

● E.g. do you feel pain, fear and anger?
● Do you feel helpless?
● Do you feel responsible, guilty or embarrassed?
● Do you anticipate successfully overcoming this setback?

3. Identify what you can do to manage your feelings about the event

● Can you let your feelings out, be prepared to be helpless and vulnerable and in other people's control?
● Can you learn from how other people have coped?
● Can you identify aspects of your problems that you can control yourself, such as feeding yourself, learning to do relaxation exercises to reduce the effect of stress on your heart as it heals?

4. Identify how you can bolster your health and well-being

For example, after the first two or three days of complete rest are over:

● Relax to ease the pain and reduce your reliance on pain medication.
● Do 'normal' activities such as dictating instructions or managing home or work problems in order to remind yourself and others that you are not just a passive patient but a person who will eventually be able to look after themselves again.
● Take emotional breaks from being a patient and under threat, by joking, by allowing yourself to take time out to enjoy talking about normal activities and people unrelated to your hospital stay.

Managing predictable and controllable life events

Looking back over the past two to three weeks, you may be able to pick out several events which you knew would happen, and over which you may have tried to exert some control. These may be everyday events such as your car or a domestic applicance breaking down, a holiday, a visit from a relative or a distant friend. Or it may be less ordinary such as a trip to an exotic part of the world, an offer of a new job or a pregnancy. These events may be welcomed, or seen as potentially threatening or stressful.

However, because they *were* predictable, you probably had more chances of being able to plan and therefore control your response and maybe even control when, or if, the event occurred. For each event, you may learn how to improve on your stress-coping techniques by seeing how well you coped at each stage. Taking one event which did stress you, for example, chest pain while shopping, ask yourself to:

1. Identify all aspects of the event which cause you to feel stressed/not stressed
- It will hurt.
- I will have to stop suddenly and I may look foolish.
- It will remind me that I am sick.

2. Identify the personal impact of the event
- I'll feel hurt and embarrassed, a failure.

3. Identify what you can do to manage your feelings about the event
- Decide if it is *rational* to believe you have failed?
- Is it likely other people will notice?
- Does it matter if other people notice?

4. Identify what you can do to change the situation
Either: To stop it happening at all by *avoidance* or by prevention; or: To act to minimize how it will affect you.

For example, if you were planning to go shopping and knew you sometimes get chest pain if you walk fast or get flustered by other people jostling you, you could:

- Either: Get someone else to do the shopping (avoidance). Walk more slowly, use the rapid relaxation exercise in Chapter 7 before and during walking, go shopping at less crowded times or to less crowded places.

DAY/TIME	ACTIVITY	STRESS 0-5 0=none 5=most severe	ANGINA 0-5 0=none 5=most severe	GTN
Example WEDS. 7.30-8.00	Getting up, got washed. Did relaxation. Got dressed.	0	0	
8.00-8.30	Breakfast, row with daughter.	3	4	✓
8.30-9.00	Late for work	1	2	
9.00-9.30	Met colleague	0	0	
9.30-10.00	Took a rest while opening mail at work. Phone off the hook. Short relaxation.	0	0	
10.00-10.30 etc.	Meeting — OK	2	0	

Fig 15: Stress and angina diary

● Or: If you feel chest pain coming on, stop, look into a shop window as if you are window-shopping or trying to get your bearings, and do the rapid relaxation to ease the chest pain, talk sense to yourself to stop yourself feeling embarrassed that some people might be looking at you.

The same four-step approach can be used with other predictable events once you know there is a pattern to them. By using a simple stress and angina diary (see Fig 15) you will find there are patterns to your stress, and many of the stressful events can be avoided, or planned for and so controlled and coped with.

Stress at work

Work is a source of stimulation, pleasure of accomplishment, material reward and social worth. It is also a potential source of demands which can lead to stress:

1. The physical conditions, including excessive stimulation from noise, light, tastes and smells, hazards and pollutants, and the pace of work itself, and the likely personal cost of mistakes.

2. The 'point' of work: whether the 'goal posts' are clear and fixed or vague and changing.

3. The use of time: how far are you able to predict your workload, use time according to your agreed priorities, and fend off interruptions and crises that upset your work rhythm?

4. Personal relationships: how much privacy is there, and how much opportunity for social contact, for professional and personal support? Are there frequent conflicts and rivalries? Do you have to deal with people, such as the public, over whom you have little control?

Each of these aspects of work which contribute to stress have elements which can be tackled according to whether they are unpredictable, uncontrollable or avoidable.

Techniques such as job analysis, time management, role analysis and personal effectiveness at work are beyond the scope of this book. But because stress in the workforce is a key factor in reducing productivity, many large organizations run courses for their employees on these topics. There is much you can do for yourself by further study of the introductory texts listed on page 199.

However, Chapter 5, which examines how you as a person may contribute to your stress, will give you some further ideas on how some of the person-to-person causes of stress may be partly caused by your own personal coping style or personality.

Summary and action points

1. **Everyday hassles** and **major life events** can occur to anyone. They become stressful when too many events occur together, making too many demands upon coping resources.

Also, the meaning of the event can determine whether it is seen as a threat or an opportunity for that person.

2. **Predictable** and **unavoidable** events such as bankruptcy, or many of the physical environmental hazards of work, are best tackled by identifying how this event will affect you both positively and negatively, and planning to cope with the negative feelings about the impact of the event, bolstering your health and allowing yourself time off away from the stressful event.

3. **Unpredictable** and **unavoidable** life crises can also be tackled in the same way once the event has happened. Additional strategies of sharing feelings and asking others for support are crucial in how people deal with major personal disasters.

4. **Predictable** and **controllable** events happen to us daily. Understanding the often conflicting priorities of work and clarifying what is expected of you, as well as time management techniques, can help increase the predictability of stressful events and enable you to either avoid the events entirely, or minimize their impact upon you.

CHAPTER 5

Angina and stressful personal styles

Who is most vulnerable to stress? It is true that the overload caused by the sheer number of life events and hassles a person faces at any one time does put strains on the person's capacity to cope as shown in Chapter 4?

But there is more to knowing who will be prone to stress than these two factors. If you look at the other patients waiting to see your family doctor or specialist, you may notice how different people react to the same potentially stressful event:

Dean sits in the waiting room for five minutes and gets up and paces about. He goes outside for a cigarette but soon comes back, having stamped it out half-smoked, worried he might miss his place in the queue. He fidgets, grinds his teeth, and scratches his leg and arm. He thinks about how he hates being unable to drive his heavy goods vehicle after his heart attack and blames his heart attack on his employer for overworking him. He clenches his fist often and walks up and down. One of the other patients who had shared the recovery ward with him tries to talk to him now, but he snaps at him to mind his own business. He goes into the consultation tense and fails to remember to ask the doctor the questions he had been saving up about whether he can take up cycling.

Graham sits behind his newspaper. He stretches out to relax and closes his eyes, planning what he will ask the doctor, then moving on to think about what plans he can make for the weekend. He feels relaxed and in control.

Pauline is sitting quietly, but close observation shows she is chewing her nails while sorting through her briefcase and her diary, reading for a few minutes, making notes, and looking at her watch every 3 or 4 minutes and sighing. She drums her fingers on her files, and begins to tear some scrap paper into shreds. She is thinking 'What a waste of time! I could have been at the office and finished my report, or have got my shopping on the way here if I'd known I'd be late. This is infuriating. I'm sure I could have got the report done and beaten our rivals to that account.'

People differ in their well-ingrained habits of seeing the world in a threatening or more challenging and positive way (their personality) and in the ways in which they decide to cope with a new stressful event. People also vary in their ability to communicate their needs and demands to others (assertiveness) and in the amount that others will support them (social support). This chapter will help you to assess your strengths and weaknesses on these components of your personal style. You can then consider for yourself whether you should make some of the suggested changes to reduce your stress potential.

Personality

In the above examples, the personalities of the people determined how they reacted to the same event. The extent to which each has found a coping strategy that works will determine how stressful they feel. Dean has a hostile personality and has not found a way to channel his aggressive thoughts. Graham does not need to make an effort to cope, as he is a relaxed, unruffled type. Pauline is an impatient and competitive person, for whom waiting time is almost painful.

This section of the chapter aims to help you to clarify which personality types are most like you, and therefore how vulnerable to stress you are. However, this chapter will also emphasize the ways in which once you understand your personality type, you can improve the ways that you cope.[1]

It is a convenient myth that a person cannot change their personality. Or as the sayings go 'A leopard cannot change his spots' and 'You can't teach an old dog new tricks'. These myths are convenient only because they give a person a perfect excuse for not making any changes at all. Yet any married couple will acknowledge that their and their partner's personalities have changed in some ways but not others over the years. It is possible to value what is healthy and be wary about situations that may feed into your weaknesses. In this way, you can modify, if not completely rebuild, your personality so you can look after yourself, cope with stress and so cope better with your angina.

Type A behaviour

The relationship between coronary heart disease and Type A behaviour profile was introduced in Chapter 1. While it may be of interest to know if your stress-prone behaviour pattern may have contributed to the development of your heart disease, it is even more important to know whether you are 'stress-prone' *NOW* because the evidence reviewed in Chapter 1 shows that those who have had coronary disease (particularly a heart attack), are more likely to develop further complications if they continue to behave in a stress-prone way.[2]

What is Type A behaviour

Behavioural style
- Explosive speech, accentuating words unnecessarily
- Frequently not ending sentences
- Cutting in on others' speech
- Turning your own or others' speech to your own interests
- Moving, walking, eating rapidly
- Getting up after meals, and getting on with the next activity
- Avoidance of waiting, queues or lines
- Doing two or more things at the same time
- Being preoccupied with doing worthwhile things
- Having few interests outside home or work
- Scheduling more and more into less and less time
- Tendency to challenge others and find their weak points
- Using aggressive gestures like clenching fists, banging on the table for emphasis
- Always setting goals for self and others
- Concerned to avoid being late for appointments
- Ambitious and concerned to show to others the evidence of success

Perhaps the best judge of whether you are Type A or not is the judgement of other people, since it is often very difficult to see one's own behavioural style objectively. But it is possible to identify the main personality traits which underpin these behaviours, and identify ways of changing them.

The underlying personality of a Type A person can be reduced to time urgency, competitiveness, and joyless striving. Each of these will be examined in detail. In addition, hostility is an important factor in Type A behaviour; it is also a strong predictor of which patients will develop severe angina.

Even if you are not a particularly competitive, time urgent and driven, striving person, it is particularly important to examine whether you are high on hostility and how well you control your anger. Finally, a fifth characteristic of Type A is the excess responsibility factor, which is related to how well you can assert and communicate your needs and beliefs. The remedy to the problem of excess responsibility is to develop assertiveness. It is an important antidote to stress for everybody but particularly for people with a tendency to take responsibility for themselves and others. The following section takes each personal style in turn, examines how to detect it, how it affects you and others, and what you can do to make a healthier personal style for yourself.

Time pressure

Do you have a 'stop-watch mentality'? Chronic impatience can become a sign of a person whose short fuse is too readily lit, and the timebomb of acute illness or other personal crisis is never far away. Your response to the following statements will help you to assess if you are the type of person for whom time is in short supply.

- 'I feel there is never enough time to do all the things I feel I should do in one day.'
- 'After eating I generally like to get up and get on with things straight away.'
- 'When driving I like to dodge through traffic to avoid queues or lines.'
- 'I get restless if I have to join a queue or line.'
- 'I try to avoid queues or lines at all costs.'
- 'I'm generally early or on time for an appointment.'
- 'I like to have a good many activities to do each day.'
- 'I like to pack in as much as I can in my leisure time.'
- 'I get irritated if someone is a minute or so late for appointments with me for no good reason.'
- 'I will change lines in supermarkets or other queues in order to avoid unnecessary waiting.'

How does being time pressured affect you?

Some people feel anxious if they have too many deadlines to meet and too many activities to do at once, while others get a 'buzz' from having a little more 'push' or 'demand' on them, thriving on the increased arousal and excitement that the challenge brings. The challenge may have the possible benefits of 'better performance under fire', tinged with the excitement of possible failure.

However, even if you respond well in the short term, a habit of setting ever more deadlines and time pressures can have long term damaging effects. First, research by Selye (1986; see Chapter 3) shows that long-term demand with few breaks leads to chronic overactivation of the physiological stress response, leading to stress disorders, general fatigue, and in particular to triggering of angina attacks. Secondly, there are the real possibilities of failure and the disappointment and blow to your self-esteem which this may bring. In the longer term, a sense of futility can build up where there is little satisfaction with carrying out activities, only with achieving the end points. Hobbies such as jogging or hillwalking can become a source of frustration if the main aim is to decrease the time taken to complete a circuit. A time-conscious person is also a source of anxiety and even displeasure to others. If you seem to be more concerned with punctuality and with speeding up what people say to you, you may seem to be putting little value on *their* time, and on what they have to say to you.

What can you do about being time pressured?

Handling deadlines
Step 1: Work out if your deadlines are:
● self-imposed or imposed by others?
● immovable or fixed?
● Do you have adequate time to reach the deadline?
● What will happen if you don't make the deadline, or postpone it?

Try listing your deadlines over the next few days in Fig 16.

Step 2: Using your list, try to see which deadlines are unnecessary, which are avoidable with little danger of bad effects; cut these deadlines out.
With unavoidable, important deadlines, try to plan realistically

Deadline	Self-imposed Yes/No	Fixed Yes/No	What may happen if you miss the deadline?	PLAN for how to (a) avoid the deadline, (b) plan realistically to meet the deadline, (c) plan for overshooting the deadline
Home e.g. Get the car through road worthiness test	No	Yes – car road test runs out in 2 weeks	I have to take the car off the road	I will get it tested but I will book it in now, in case it fails and needs work. If I'm late, I'll have to get the bus for a few days.
Work				
Others				

Fig 16: Deadlines diary

how you will meet them. For example, give yourself more time than usual to prepare for them.

Step 3: Get used to letting unimportant deadlines pass; decide which deadline you will over-shoot. See how easy it is next time to let yourself off these unimportant deadlines.

Step 4: For important, unavoidable deadlines, see if you can make a real effort to plan in advance. For example, if you normally drive or walk from home to the shops or work in a certain time, start off 5 or 10 minutes earlier. Drive or walk more slowly, occasionally take a 'scenic' route and enjoy the travelling itself.

Step 5: Look back on your list after a few days and see how easy or difficult it was to:
- avoid deadlines
- let deadlines slip
- plan for important deadlines.

Using time rather than letting time use you
Try to schedule *fewer* activities each day and see how much *more* you achieve by doing them well. See also how much more satisfaction you can get from doing a job well rather than simply finishing it.

Try to reduce your clock watching. Discipline yourself to allow enough time to get to places. When you are travelling, concentrate on enjoying the journey itself, or distract yourself by listening to music, talking to people, or doing a relaxation exercise.

Take 'time off' breaks
If you are the type of person who takes days rather than hours to unwind on holiday, you can train yourself to switch off more rapidly and more effectively if you routinely give yourself mini-time breaks. This means having periods of time when you have no clocks or watches and you make an effort to lose your sense of time. Because you may need to end your 'time break', or your deep relaxation exercise (which can encourage you to lose your sense of time), set a clock or ask someone to remind you when your time-free period is up.

Remember
'It is better to arrive in good shape, than not to arrive at all!'
'More haste, less speed!'

Mark Twain said 'Never put off 'til tomorrow what you can do the day after tomorrow.'

Joyless striving

Are you always busy, on the go with many projects at once? Do you set high standards for yourself even in your leisure activities? Do you often reset your goals when you achieve them so you have to work even harder next time?

The questions below will help you to assess if you have this trait within your personality:

- Do you feel that you *should* be doing something more worthwhile when you are doing something trivial such as watching TV?
- Do you tend to watch serious documentaries, news and current events on TV rather than light programmes like soaps and comedies?
- Do you feel you *should* be watching more serious TV, or reading the paper, or doing something useful round the house?
- When you take up a new hobby, do you try to do it really well? Do you try to be better at your hobby than others?
- Do other people who only do 'unimportant' jobs or hobbies annoy you?
- Does it annoy you if others do things less well than you would, or don't seem to try hard enough?
- Do you have feelings of being trapped by the many activities you should be doing?
- When at home, do you often find yourself thinking and talking about your work?
- Do you often feel you have to do something tangible every day in order to feel good about yourself?
- Do you like to have many projects on the go at any one time?
- Do you lose interest in finishing off projects and feel keener to start new ones?

How does 'joyless striving' affect you?

A single-minded pursuit of a goal, despite setbacks and distractions, is a sensible strategy for success. But it can become a habit if applied to all areas of your life. For example, if you decide to take up a new hobby such as the card game bridge, it may well improve your performance to go to lessons, buy books and magazines, keep a diary of your successes and failures and practise the game five nights a week. but it could become an obsession rather than a form of relaxation!

If you answered 'yes' to many of the above questions, you are showing signs of having the coping style known as 'joyless striving'. You have a strong need to be involved in constructive and worthwhile activities. This is because your view of how much you value yourself is made up of what you *do* rather than what you *are*. So, to you, doing things at only 'half cock' is a sign of weakness. You may think that other people will think less of you if you don't succeed at everything, even how well you trim the lawn, or prepare the meal at Christmas, or how you drive the car! If you have many projects on the go, and fill your work and home time with goals to be achieved, there is little room for enjoyment of the *process* of achieving the goals. If when you achieve a goal you reset your sights higher, you are always pushing yourself, and you never seem to enjoy the achievement of success since there are always higher pinnacles to climb. You will be putting yourself under constant pressure in the same way as a person who runs their life around deadlines. It may also affect your social relationships since this style of 'joyless striving' can make you seem very serious-minded and even superior to others. Your behaviour may bore other people and be a barrier to their relaxation as they may feel that you judge them to be wasting your time, and wasting their own time by engaging in less serious activities. Ironically, you are likely to be *less* efficient than other people, since you are probably trying too hard at even unimportant activities, rather than saving your effort and concentration for the most important tasks.

How can you change your 'joyless striving'?

● Spot the times when you seem to be needlessly competing with yourself or others.
● Try to do some rather unimportant, trivial activities just for the pleasure of doing it, not for how you think others will think of you. For example, try taking up a hobby that nobody else knows about and let it be enjoyable for itself, and try to resist telling others how well you are doing until you feel sure that

you know you are enjoying it for its own sake.
- Try to do something trivial that other people will see you doing, but do it only as well as it needs to be done, not to impress yourself or others.
- Remember, the person who said 'If a job is worth doing, it's worth doing well' probably spent so long doing things well, he or she forgot how to do things for the fun of it!

Competitiveness

Do you compare yourself to other people who seem to have 'flashy' lifestyles with all the hallmarks of success such as fast cars, big houses, attractive spouses and with many trophies to their success in their office or home? Do you constantly measure your self-worth against how well your performance or appearance matches with those of others? Answers to the questions below will help you to measure your 'achievement ethic':

- Do you feel that you should always be striving to push yourself to meet new challenges and develop new skills?
- Do you feel that you are what you do?
- Do you feel you should always strive to achieve more, however well you have done before?
- Do you agree that 'If at first you don't succeed try, try, again' is a good personal motto?
- Do you admire and want to be like people who have done well, or become rich or famous?
- Do you disagree with the phrase 'It's lonely at the top' because you believe that people will want to know you if you are successful?
- Do you believe there are always winners and losers and you are resolved to be a winner?
- Are you distrustful of other people who may become better performers than you?

How does competitiveness affect you?

If you agree with most of the above statements, you probably have a high need for achievement. This attitude is encouraged in our society. Television, radio and newspapers are often full of success stories. *But* success does not always bring happiness.

There are always plenty of stories of how former stars have been unhappy and even suicidal when they found that fame did not bring happiness. And even at an everyday level, there are many ways in which we can see that striving for success will not guarantee happiness, and that constant striving which continues even after a realistic level of success has already been achieved, can lead to frustration and despair.

The long-term effect on your health of constant competition is the same as for people who suffer time pressure and joyless striving, since all three traits lead to constant overdemand and chronic activation of the stress response. The longer-term effect on your personal relationships and emotional well-being is also destructive.

Competitiveness leads to superficial relationships with little trust or warmth or caring, since all that is valued are your actions, not yourself. Other people will feel threatened and may withdraw from you, or attack your weaknesses. They may distrust you as someone who uses other people as stepping stones to your success. This 'machiavellian' behaviour is often irritating to subordinates and threatening to superiors. You may be attractive to people who will make use of your success and strengths but will not value you when you fail or become vulnerable. Your relationships will lack emotional warmth and support, which no amount of material or social success can compensate for in the long run.

What can you do to modify your competitiveness?

One of the keys to conquering competitiveness is to learn to set your *own* standards for achievement, rather than always trying to set your standards by what you think other people will value you for achieving.

Step 1: Examine your standards
Try to check back over your main activities in the last few days and see what you expect of yourself. Are you setting your standards higher than you need to?

Step 2: Learn to get away with less than perfection
Try to decide for activities in the near future, just how much you need to do:

a) in order to get away with it

b) to do it to your own satisfaction.

If there is a big gap between a) and b) pick a couple of activities, and decide you will do them only to level a). Write these down in your diary or calendar.

Then check back when you have done them that you stuck to your resolution. Ask yourself, 'Did it matter that you only did it in order to get away with it'?

In future, try to pick out activities you don't have to do so well and let yourself 'get away with it more'. You may be surprised to find that you can let up on some things and still feel a worthwhile person.

Step 3: Reward yourself when you ease up on some achievements

Every time you catch yourself setting needlessly high goals for yourself, let yourself off the hook and congratulate yourself!

Put reminders to yourself in key places. For example, a red dot or biro mark in your diary at work can indicate to you a warning to examine your standards. This could be useful at the point in a meeting where you examine your diary in order to see where you can fit in more work. By looking at the warning red dot, you could stop to ask yourself whether you are simply taking on more to meet your own high standards or in order to look more capable than everyone else!

Step 4: Take on hobbies or activities you don't have to achieve at

See what activities you do now just for pleasure. See how much more time you could spend on them.

Remember: People who feel they *have* to achieve at everything often believe there is not enough money, status, power and regard from others to go round, so they fight for it. This is not true. You can get enough of what you really need to survive comfortably without stepping on others to get there.

Hostility

A study of 255 male medical students, followed up 25 years afterwards found those who had hostile personalities were more likely to develop angina.[3] At Duke University in Durham, USA, 307 men and 117 women underwent angiography to investigate angina. They found that the amount of blockage (atherosclerosis) in the coronary arteries was *less* likely to predict who was most disabled by angina than how hostile they were.[4] So, modifying how hostile you are may reduce your symptoms.

Being hostile can mean you are easily provoked to become angry. Anger is an emotion, like anxiety, which is justified in some circumstances but not others. It is healthy to express anger if you are thwarted in achieving your legitimate goals or meeting your everyday needs. But a person who has a hostile personality is not simply anger-prone: they have a view of the world which can lead to chronic stress due to frequent angry outbursts and to brittle relationships which are distrustful and emotionally shallow.

Do you believe such things as:

● 'If I don't stand up for myself, someone else will get what I want'
● 'You just can't trust people'
● 'People today are just not as moral as they should be'
● 'Other people just don't care as much as I do, and they should!'
● 'If I don't watch my back, someone will be getting one over on me' or
● 'I feel others are out to get me, or put me down'?

Do you generally feel:

● like hitting someone?
● that you get into arguments easily?
● you have problems controlling your temper?
● Do you tend to shout, swear, throw things, clench your fists, hit out, slam doors?
● Do you drive impatiently or aggressively, hooting your horn if you can't pass a slow driver, or signalling your displeasure at bad drivers?
● Do you get into races or 'cut up' other drivers?

If so, you have a tendency to express your anger. But there are also hostile people who do get angry, but bottle up their anger. Do you generally:

- have angry thoughts about people? Feel easily annoyed and frustrated?
- sit and fume about what has annoyed you?
- turn over and over in your mind how you would like to get revenge?

How does hostility affect you?

We may all feel strongly about some issues and many people have strong moral, religious or political views. But if you hang on to beliefs in the face of evidence that your beliefs are incorrect in the present situation, or let other people provoke you for the fun of seeing you rise to bait, or you generally feel people are out to do you harm, you may well have a hostility problem.

You may develop problems of anger control because you are easily provoked by situations that do not provoke other people.

If you are often angry, and express it in aggressive language and acts, you will experience strong physiological arousal since anger expression is often accompanied by very sudden increases in heart rate and blood pressure – anger is the emotion most likely to trigger angina. Not only will it affect you physically, but aggressive language and behaviour will threaten other people who may retaliate, or withdraw from you, or in other ways seek to do you down, and so proving to you that the world is against you!

If you sit on your anger, you may not threaten others directly, but if you harbour aggressive thoughts about others this will harm your relationship with them and make you distrustful and emotionally cold. This in turn can lead others to be less open with you, and add to your cynical and distrustful view of the world.

What can you do about hostility and anger?

You were not born with a short fuse. You have learned a habit of seeing the world in a hostile way and you have learned to produce an angry response.

Understanding what makes you angry

1. **Personal insult,** particularly being sworn at by other people, is a common anger trigger.
2. **Thwarting your goals:** stopping you doing things that are important to you, such as a car mechanic not fixing your car so you are unable to go away on holiday on time.

DESCRIBE THE ANGER PROVOKING EVENT	WHAT TYPE OF ANGER PROVO-CATION WAS IT? (personal insult, thwarting your goals, frustration with others, threat to your values)	HOW ANGRY DID YOU GET? 0 – not at all angry 1 – mildly angry 2 – very angry 3 – extremely angry
E.g. The car wasn't mended and I had to take it back to the garage again.	Frustrations with others (the mechanic). Thwarting my goals (I wanted to go on holiday today in the car).	2 – very angry!

Fig 17: Anger provocation exercise

3. Frustration with others who do not let you achieve your goals. Children are often an enormous source of frustration to parents who cannot see why they are disobedient.

4. Threat or **insult** to people or values important to you: for example, party political broadcasts of a party you do not vote for which presents ideas and values opposite to your own, may be a source of annoyance.

Using the Anger Provocation Exercise Sheet (Fig 17) record over the next week the type of provoking events you faced. In the first column, describe the situation. In the second, put which of the four reasons outlined above (personal insult, thwarting your goals, frustration with others, threat to your values) seems to explain why you got provoked. In the final column, rate how angry you became.

Over a period of days or weeks you can determine which situations regularly make you angry. This knowledge can be useful in helping you to understand how your views of the world lead you to become more easily provoked to anger than other people. Using the same way of recording your thoughts as in Chapter 3, Table 3, you can find out for yourself if there are some circumstances in which you are becoming angry because you have jumped to the wrong conclusions. Asking others whom you respect as being better able to control their emotions than yourself how they would have reacted, can also help you to understand your anger reaction and learn to change your thoughts about anger-provoking events.[4]

Using the sequence in Fig 18 you can see how your thoughts about the anger-provoking event, your bodily arousal and your behaviour can feed into each other to produce an angry out-

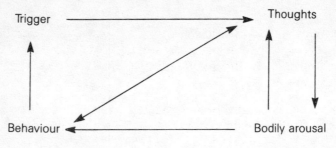

After Novaco, R.W. (1979)[5]

Fig 18: Anger provocation

burst. It is well known that thinking angry thoughts can provoke strong physiological arousal. The bodily sensations of the adrenalin response can become a cue to remind you that you are aroused and that this arousal is associated with fighting and attacking behaviour. It can become almost automatic for a person in this situation to respond to the bodily cues of arousal by bracing themselves. Their behaviour and posture can indicate aggression, by for example, 'squaring up' to the other person and getting close to them with threatening gestures and a loud tone of voice. This behaviour itself can be a cue for the thoughts to become more aggressive. The vicious circle is complete, with the thoughts, bodily arousal, and behaviour interacting to produce an angry outburst.

The Anger Inoculation Training, derived from the Stress model used on page 54 can be used to overcome this vicious circle.

The key to this approach is to take each episode stage by stage, and to control your thoughts, bodily arousal and behaviour at each phase.

Stage 1: Preparing for provocation
Your thoughts: Using the information you have gleaned from the anger provocation exercise, identify in advance the situations and people who tend to provoke you. Try to think of the thoughts you have which make you feel angry. See if you can substitute more calming thoughts:

- 'This could be a rough situation, but I know how to deal with it.'
- 'I can work out a plan to handle this. Easy does it.'
- 'Remember, stick to the issues and don't take it personally.'
- 'There is no need for an argument, I shall just state my case.'

Your bodily arousal and behaviour: It is important to remain calm and physically relaxed, breathing slowly and evenly, and maintaining a non-threatening posture and a low and calm tone of voice.

Stage 2: Confronting the situation
Your thoughts: Learn to distance yourself from the provocation so you will not overreact:

- 'OK, so you seem to be rather rude but it's not worth taking it personally.'

- 'He's entitled to his views, so what?'
- 'If I stay calm, I'll handle it better.'
- 'I don't need to prove myself. Don't make more out of this than I have to.'
- 'There is no point getting angry, think of what I have to do to get out of this.'
- 'Look for the positive side and don't jump to conclusions.'

Bodily arousal and behaviour: It is particularly important to maintain a relaxed calm stance, low and unthreatening voice and to maintain your distance in order to prevent the other person from feeling threatened and retaliating.

Stage 3: Coping with your physical tension
Your thoughts:
- 'My muscles are tight, I feel sick. I can counteract this by relaxing and slowing down.'
- 'Take this problem point by point. There must be a better way to react than getting angry.'
- 'My muscles are getting tight. Relax and slow things down.'
- 'My anger is a sign of what I need to do. Time for problem solving.'
- 'He probably wants me to get angry but I'm going to deal with it my own way.'

Bodily arousal and behaviour: A positive effort to back off and remain calm will be a cue to yourself, as well as to other people involved, that you are not getting worked up.

Stage 4: Reviewing your performance
A. If a conflict is unresolved:
Thoughts:
- 'Forget about the aggravation. Thinking about it only makes me upset.'
- 'Try to shake it off. Don't let it interfere with what I'm going to do.'
- 'Relaxation is better than anger.'
- 'Don't take it personally. It's probably not so serious.'

It is important to try to put the situation behind you and do not let your anger or frustration eat you up.

Bodily arousal and behaviour:
Try to do something that will help release the tension constructively such as taking brisk physical exercise or doing a relaxation exercise.

B. If the conflict is resolved:

Thoughts:

Congratulate yourself!

- 'My pride can get me into trouble, but I'm learning to overcome it.'
- 'I'm so pleased I got through that without blowing up.'
- 'I handled that one pretty well. That's doing a good job.'

Bodily tension and behaviour:

You may still feel somewhat tense even though you have succeeded in controlling yourself. Again, it is worth taking some brief physical exercise or doing a relaxation response to get rid of this tension.

In order to practise these techniques it can help to go over recent events in your mind. Use the situations you have listed using the Anger Provocation Exercise sheet (Fig 17):

1. List the situations which regularly provoke you.
2. Put them into an order from LEAST to MOST provoking.
3. Identify which type of provocation this is (threat to others, threat to your values, threat to your possessions, personal insult, frustration with others, thwarting your goals).
4. Starting with the least provoking event take yourself through the situations using the four-step 'anger inoculation method'.

You can also use the anger inoculation method next time you feel you are being unnecessarily aggressive or becoming wound up. This technique was used by a psychologist, Raymond Novaco,[5] from the USA. It has been used with people who have particularly short fuses, such as people who have been violent offenders, as well as people who develop health problems when they are in acute stress, including people who develop angina pain when angry.

The anger inoculation technique can be used to help you plan for situations which you know are often likely to provoke you to anger. When you have been through such a situation using the anger control techniques, it can be helpful to look back over the situation and try to find out how you responded and see if there are better solutions to your response. Fig 19 gives an example of how you can plan for yourself better solutions by tackling your reaction to the trigger, your thoughts, your bodily feelings and your behaviour as separate but interacting responses.

Fig 19: Anger inoculation training example

Trigger	**Solution**
Coming home most evenings from work and finding your partner, who leaves for work after you, still hasn't cleaned up his/her clothes from the bedroom floor nor cleared the breakfast table.	'There is a time and a place for tackling this problem – when we are both not tired.'
Thoughts	
'I hate this! What a slob! Am I supposed to deal with this? Doesn't she/he care about me any more? Selfish pig . . .'	'If I get worked up, I'll only turn it into a row. I'll try to focus on the problem in hand.'
Bodily feelings	
Tension in stomach. Clenched fists, tight jaw. Beginning of headache.	'If I stay calm I'll be in control. Relax!'
Behaviour	
Stamping around the house, shouting at anyone, throwing clothes out of bedroom, crashing crockery in kitchen, let rip when partner comes in.	'Sit still. Put your hands in your lap – unclench your fists/sit on them! Talk calmly, slowly, lower your voice.'

Excessive responsibility

Do you feel a large amount of responsibility rests on your shoulders? Are you generally rather sensible and serious, often overburdened and tired? To see if you are prone to taking excessive amounts of responsibility for others, see how many of these questions you answer 'yes' to:

● Do you think of yourself as serious, sensible and responsible?

- Do you distrust others who may not be as good at doing things as you?
- Do you get anxious when other people have to do your work or activities?
- Do you hover around checking other people are doing things as well as you would?
- Is it a sign of weakness to give work to others that you could do yourself?
- Is it a sign of weakness to have to ask for help?
- Do you feel that others who try to share their work or home responsibility are shirking their responsibilities?
- Do you find it difficult to get others to take on their own responsibilities?
- Do you often feel tired, overburdened and harried?

If you answered 'yes' to many of the above questions, you are likely to experience considerable stress. This is because you are taking responsibility for just about everything that happens around you. This is known as the '*Atlas Syndrome*'. If you remember from your school days, Atlas was a giant who had to shoulder all the weight of the world. Naturally, feeling responsible for your work and for others' activities will eventually put you under stress. Of course, you have to be responsible for some of your actions and duties such as caring for children or doing necessary parts of your job, but just how far you take responsibility *unnecessarily* is the key to this problem.

If you suffer from excessive responsibility you are a person who has difficulty defining your own self-worth. You may also find it difficult to define exactly what you are responsible for, and the rights and duties of others. This can lead to problems in assertiveness, which can be expressed as either submissiveness or aggressiveness. You may have difficulty defining your own needs and expressing your needs to others. You will be seen by other people as 'all business and no play', humourless and 'bearing the weight of the world on your shoulders'. You may also be seen by others as interfering or unnecessarily controlling, or simply 'a mug' for taking on all the dirty work. If you rarely delegate activities to others and appear not to respect the abilities of others to cope, people may be jealous of you and feel their own abilities are overlooked by you. You are likely to be a lonely, chronically tired and unhappy person since you have not learned how to share either your pleasures or your chores. This style of behaviour is often maintained until you crack under the strain, because it is often convenient for other people to heap responsibility onto such a 'workhorse'. However, when under pressure you finally decide to give some responsibility to other people, they may not react as readily as you would, which can add to your resentment and a worsening of your relationships at a time when you most need support.

What can you do to modify your tendency to take excessive responsibility?

Step 1: Defining your roles
Write down your main roles, that is, how you describe yourself to people who don't know you.

For example, 'my roles are:
Spouse, breadwinner, mother, dog lover.'

Write down how other people see you in these roles, the good and the bad qualities!

For example:

> *'Breadwinner'*   capable
> hardworking
> stingy

Now decide if there are any roles which are so unrewarding that you feel you could give them up. For the other roles, write down what is the minimum you could do to 'get away with it' and on the right-hand side write down what you do now.

For example:

Get away with it	What I do now
'Dog lover' Feed and exercise the dog. Take it to the vet when ill.	All of this, but also take other people's dogs out, feed strays, go to dog shows.
'Breadwinner' – *salesman* Do 20 sales a week.	30–40 sales a week. Work in evenings on paperwork.

Write down for each role what you can give up or 'delegate', that is, give to someone else to do.

For example:

Minimum I have to do	What I can delegate, give up
'Dog lover'	
Feed and exercise my dog.	I won't go to dog shows.
Take it to the vet.	I'll get my son to look after the dog, and exercise it at weekends.
	I won't look after other people's dogs.
'Breadwinner' – *salesman*	
Have to make 20 sales a week	I don't have to go for extra sales over 20 a week.
	I can give a lot of the clerical work to the secretary.
	If I don't get the work done during the day, I won't take it home.

When you have done this exercise, you may realize you can reduce your stress by taking on less, by only doing the minimum necessary to please yourself or by giving up unnecessary tasks to others.

Remember:
Winston Churchill said 'The price of greatness is responsibility' and not all of us need to be great at everything to be happy.

D. Piatt said 'The man is great who can use the brains of others to carry out his work.'

Step 2: Learn to be more assertive
In order to be able to 'stick to your guns' over what is and what is not your responsibility, it is important to develop your assertiveness. We all have needs, rights and duties towards others. Inevitably, as we try to fulfil our needs we come into conflict with others. Whether you tackle these conflicts in an assertive, a passive or aggressive way, will influence both whether your needs are met and whether others' needs are met.

When you are *aggressive*, you put your own needs first and ignore others.

When you are *passive* you put others' needs before your own.

When you are *assertive* you put your own needs first, but respect other people's needs also.

The effects of being passive are generally to encourage others to take advantage of you. They may find you easygoing at first, but will rarely respect or trust you since you are unable to stand up for what you believe in.

The effects of being aggressive have been touched on under 'hostility', and include increasing fear and distrust and potential for revenge of others towards you.

The effects of being assertive are that others respect your views and may be prepared to go some way to share problems and duties since you can be trusted to be honest about your capabilities.

Below are some examples of scenes using different styles of behaviour. In each scene decide whether A is being assertive, passive or aggressive:

SCENE (1)
A: Why do you always leave your socks lying about? You are a slob.
B: I'm no worse than you. I'll do what I like in my own house.
A: Your house? Who pays half the mortgage, you tight-fisted slob?

ASSERTIVE   PASSIVE   AGGRESSIVE

SCENE (2)
B: I want you to stay late tonight. The agenda is not ready for the monthly department meeting, but I know I can rely on you to sort it out.
A: I suppose it is important, I'd hate the meeting to go badly. Can't someone else do it?
B: I pay you to do what I tell you.
A: I know you're upset and overworked. I'll do my best.

ASSERTIVE   PASSIVE   AGGRESSIVE

SCENE (3)
B: Now we have a cut-back in staff in this department, and I'm rushed off my feet. We need to rationalize our work. I'm already taking on all the new work – can't you do more?
A: I do all the long-term cases, remember. Perhaps if you do some long-term cases and I do a day 'on take', the work will even out. But I think we have to cut back somewhere. How about if I do a day 'on take', you do a day on my cases, and we close the waiting list until we get more staff.

ASSERTIVE   PASSIVE   AGGRESSIVE

The answers are: Scene 1: Aggressive; Scene 2: Passive; Scene 3: Assertive.

Below are the main characteristics of assertive, passive and aggressive behaviour.

Assertive and unassertive behaviour

Passive behaviour	Aggressive behaviour	Assertive behaviour
CHARACTERISTICS Not true to yourself.	CHARACTERISTICS Boosting yourself at others' expense	CHARACTERISTICS True to yourself.
NON-VERBAL BEHAVIOURS Avoids eye contact, covers mouth with hand, smiles ingratiatingly or cringingly, nervous gestures.	NON-VERBAL BEHAVIOURS Staring eye contact, loud voice, sarcasm, finger pointing, patronizing tone of voice.	NON-VERBAL BEHAVIOURS Steady eye contact, steady tone of voice, clear speech.
YOUR FEELINGS Hurt, fearful, possibly depressed or resentful later.	YOUR FEELINGS Self-righteous, superior, possibly guilty later.	YOUR FEELINGS Confident, self-respecting.
OTHERS' FEELINGS FOR YOU Pity, irritation and disgust.	OTHERS' FEELINGS FOR YOU Anger, resentment.	OTHERS' FEELINGS FOR YOU Respect, liking.
OTHERS' FEELINGS FOR SELF Guilty or superior.	OTHERS' FEELINGS FOR SELF Hurt, humiliated.	OTHERS' FEELINGS FOR SELF Valued, respected.
CONSEQUENCES FOR YOU Allow others to choose for you. Do not achieve own goals.	CONSEQUENCES FOR YOU You choose for others. Achieve own goals by hurting others.	CONSEQUENCES FOR YOU You choose for self. May achieve own goals.
CONSEQUENCES FOR OTHERS Achieve their goals at expense of non-assertive person.	CONSEQUENCES FOR OTHERS Do not achieve their own goals.	CONSEQUENCES FOR OTHERS May achieve their own goals.

There are many approaches towards becoming assertive which are outlined in the further reading sections.

Most require you to be aware of your rights. The main human rights which are acknowledged as reasonable in Western society are:

- The right to consider your needs to be as important as others'.
- The right to make mistakes.
- The right to refuse requests without feeling guilty.
- The right to have your own opinions as long as it does not violate the rights of others.
- The right to have your achievements recognized.
- The right to protest if unfairly treated.
- The right to ask for help.
- The right to privacy.
- The right to judge your own behaviour, thoughts and emotions and to take responsibility for the consequences of these.

Step 3

The third step is to learn how to communicate your needs more effectively. The behaviours listed above give clues as to how to avoid the main pitfalls, but more detailed approaches are covered in several self-help books, and classes run at further education and health service departments can give you an opportunity for active practice. Recently, personnel departments of large organizations have begun to run courses for their staff, particularly women, since more assertive and open communication has been shown to be beneficial both to the staff and to the company.

And finally, the good news

So far, we have only considered personal styles and behaviours which contribute to stress and some of the antidotes. But there is evidence that some people have learned personal styles which buffer them from stress. One such style is known as Hardiness. Suzanne Kobasa, a research psychologist in New York, developed the theory that 'hardy' or 'less stress-prone' people have a personal style which expresses commitment, control and challenge. [6]

Commitment is a sense of personal mission, a belief in one's self-worth and the value of one's activities and interests.

Control is the belief that one can influence the important course of events in one's life. Explanations for events such as promotion or ill-health are sought in one's own responsibility, not in the actions of others, fate or a god.

Challenge is the individual's tolerance for change, an expectation that stability is temporary, change is normal. Further, change is viewed as a source of stimulation, opening up opportunities for growth and experimentation.

Kobasa found that middle and higher executives who showed these three characteristics tended to be fitter and healthier.

It is not yet known whether having a 'hardy' personality can protect one from further ill-effects of stress, nor of the relationship of 'hardiness' to angina. However, it is plausible that a person who feels their life has meaning, who seeks to control their life and who sees change as an opportunity rather than a crisis, will perceive few situations as threats and will learn to use a range of coping strategies to reduce the unpleasant effects and increase the positive effects of potentially stressful events in their lives.

Finally, there are indirect effects of one's personal style which can be both positive and negative. Research on the unpleasant effects of Life Events discussed in Chapter 4 showed that people who have good social support networks tend to suffer less stress during major crises.

Social support tends to be rather weak for people who have abrasive personalities, such as those with Type A characteristics, particularly competitiveness and hostility.

Social support has several functions. People can provide practical help, expert knowledge or demonstrate how you can overcome a particular problem. They are also important as a source of emotional support in bolstering your self-esteem.

Certainly, the amount and quality of social support a person has, and in particular the availability of a close and confiding relationship in times of crisis, is a well-documented stress antidote.

Planning for crises as well as the unpredictable will be more effective if you have a well-developed social support network. Chapter 11 goes further in to how to develop social support through self-help groups.

Summary

1. Personality factors of *Type A behaviour*, and its components of *time pressure, joyless striving, competitiveness, hostility* and *excessive responsibility*, each individually, and collectively, increase your vulnerability to stress.

Antidotes to these coping styles include:

Time pressure: Reducing your working to deadlines.
Having time-free mini-holidays.

Joyless striving: Reducing your high standards.
Taking up trivial or uncompetitive pursuits.

Competitiveness: Stop comparing your performance with others.
Boost your self-worth by non-competitive pursuits for the fun of it.
Go for quality, not quantity.

Hostility: Notice your anger triggers.
Break down your responses and tackle the thoughts, bodily arousal and behaviours one step at a time.

Excessive responsibility: Learn to know what is and isn't your responsibility.
Learn to be assertive in communicating your needs to others.

2. Personality factors such as *Hardiness* (Commitment, Control and Challenge) and personal relationships which provide *social support* are good to stress-proof yourself.

CHAPTER 6

Angina and stress responses

The aim of this chapter is to outline the way we react to stress. The immediate and prolonged effects of stress on our mind and body will be described. Just why these responses occur and the fact that they are the body's *natural* reaction to a threat will be emphasized. The stress response is a legacy that our ancestors have given us to help us deal with a modern, hostile environment.

Because people are so different, some of us will respond to stress in a bodily way, some will respond emotionally by getting angry or upset, and some may show stress by their behaviour, for example, smoking or drinking excessively. All of us will respond with a mixture of these ways, but usually, we are only aware of some of our responses. With a little practice we can identify our *predominant* response.

Physiological responses to stress

When you come up against a sudden, challenging situation you may notice that your heart rate speeds up, you breathe faster and less deeply and that your muscles tense. However, you can guarantee, if you are feeling these effects, that other effects are also occurring in the main systems in your body. Working from the top down we will examine the physiological stress signs. Research has shown that stress affects all of the systems in our body. The main pathway that channels the stressful stimuli from our brain to the various systems is via the nervous and the hormone systems. (For a review see Lee, 1983.)[1]

The nervous and hormone systems

The immediate responses to sudden stress occur in seconds, and are controlled by nerves which send messages from the brain to the muscles and activate glands to release hormones. These chemicals flow into the blood and they are taken to all parts of the body. The main chemicals are *adrenalin*, *noradrenalin* and *corticosteroids*. These hormones then serve to maintain the stress response by stimulating the nervous system in the same way as stressful stimuli do, causing more of their chemicals to be released. Therefore, a vicious circle is set up.

The senses

Immediately, within seconds, the senses sharpen, the pupils dilate and for a short while you may be able to take in more visual information. This is also true for hearing, smell, taste and touch sensations. But if the stress continues over time, a chronic reaction occurs and these same senses become dull, you may get blurred vision or tinnitus (ringing in the ears). Extreme stress reactions may include the temporary loss of smell or taste. The salivary glands may produce less saliva into the mouth. Most people will have experienced a dry, sticky mouth when asked to speak in public and this can be very uncomfortable.

The skin

The immediate reaction of the blood circulation to the skin is to decrease, causing the characteristic pallor of someone who is frightened. If someone is chronically stressed, this pallor may be interspersed with bouts of sweating and flushing, especially of the face, neck and chest.

The cardiovascular system

This includes the heart and blood vessels. As described above the blood vessels to the skin constrict, diverting the blood supply to the main muscles and more important parts of the body such as the internal organs. The heart rate speeds up, and some people experience palpitations and a thumping sensation in the chest which can be very unpleasant. Some people experience chest pain or other symptoms of angina. This also pushes the blood pressure up, which can cause headaches. If this state of alertness or arousal continues it can be dangerous in people who have a tendency to high blood pressure. There is also some evidence that the long-term effects of arousal on the heart and blood vessels are very damaging and may trigger a heart attack, (Williams *et al*, 1982).[2]

The respiratory system

When stressed you tend to breathe faster but less deeply and this can cause panting and overbreathing. Hyperventilation, or overbreathing, occurs when too much oxygen is taken into the lungs and they cannot do their usual job of removing the waste products – mainly carbon dioxide. Too much carbon dioxide circulating in the blood causes the brain to stimulate the lungs to breathe more in an attempt to breathe it out and so a vicious circle is set up. The symptoms of hyperventilation can include palpitations, a fast heart rate, dizziness, shortness of breath, chest pain, tingling in the lips, fingers, and/or toes, anxiety, weakness, and sometimes loss of consciousness. Dizziness and tingling appear to be the earliest warning signs. This is not dangerous but can be very unpleasant to experience. There is some research evidence to suggest hyperventilation is linked to spasm of the coronary arteries causing angina.

The digestive system

The effects of arousal on this system can be acute (immediate) or chronic (prolonged). You must have experienced an acute effect of stress, known as 'butterflies in the stomach' as it churns and empties its contents. The bowels and bladder may produce sensations of fullness creating an irresistible desire to open. Chronic stress can cause chronic loose bowels and may be a major problem. These bowel disorders will be discussed in the section on stress and illness.

The muscle system

The immediate effects of high arousal on muscles includes the surging of blood and energy into the muscles of the limbs to help them cope with a wide range of demands. At this time you may also experience tenseness, twitching and shaking in your limb muscles. However, in the longer term, the opposite effect occurs, and the muscles feel weak, tired and heavy. Many people who are chronically stressed complain of fatigue. You may also be

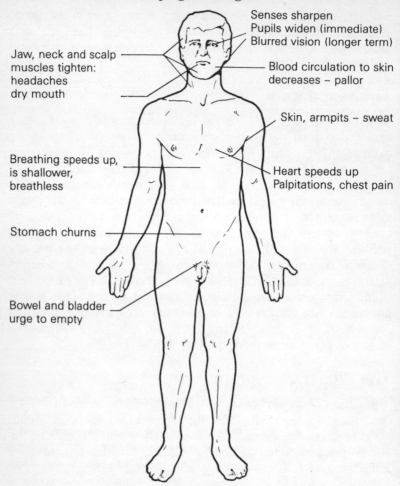

Senses sharpen
Pupils widen (immediate)
Blurred vision (longer term)

Jaw, neck and scalp muscles tighten: headaches dry mouth

Blood circulation to skin decreases – pallor

Skin, armpits – sweat

Breathing speeds up, is shallower, breathless

Heart speeds up
Palpitations, chest pain

Stomach churns

Bowel and bladder urge to empty

Your behaviour: Less co-ordinated – clumsy
Your thinking: Indecisive, fearful, jump to
                 conclusions, aggressive, withdrawn

Fig 20: The stress response

more prone to injury or tearing of the muscles, and many chronic strains or long-lasting aches and pains can be due to chronic stress. Fig 20 shows you all the major stress responses on the different systems in the body.

Case history

Mr Smith had suffered from high blood pressure for many years. This was brought to his attention after his first heart attack. He was told to learn to relax as he was demonstrating obvious signs of stress. He went to his doctor on a number of occasions complaining of sweating profusely, palpitations, loose bowels and fatigue. On the final occasion, when his blood pressure was especially high, his doctor recommended that he enrol in a relaxation class. After some thought he agreed. After just seven sessions and practising at home, some of his symptoms had disappeared and the others were much improved. Mr Smith firmly believes he averted another heart attack and now admits to leading a much more rewarding life.

Emotional responses to stress

Some people are more aware of their emotional responses to stress. Most of us from time to time will have been told by close friends or partners that we are irritable or bad-tempered when things get on top of us. But for some people the emotional response may be overwhelming and lead to further problems in coping with the events that triggered the stress response. People tend to show they are stressed in one of three ways, but these are not, of course, mutually exclusive. There is the *anxiety* response, the *hostility* response and the *depression* response.

The anxiety response

The anxiety response may show itself in one of three ways: through our *thoughts, feelings* or *behaviour*. Sometimes it can be expressed in all three ways. In addition to the physiological responses of arousal described above, there are some thoughts and feelings which are characteristic of someone who is feeling anxious. Worry and dread are classic responses for someone who is anxious. These will often describe themselves as 'a bit of a worrier' and tell you how they dread everything from the next electricity bill coming in to going on holiday in case they get burgled whilst away. Anxious people with angina will often worry about the next angina attack in case it is the one to cause a heart attack, and dread going to the post office because it sometimes brings on angina. If you are a worrier, it is very easy to form a vicious circle of worry about angina symptoms and triggering more angina. (See Fig 21.)

You may find it difficult to concentrate and little irritating

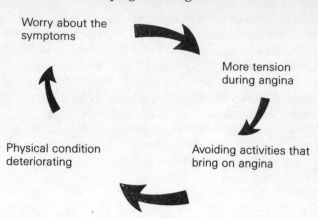

Fig 21: Worry and angina symptoms – the vicious circle

thoughts may play like a broken record in your mind. At times your mind may seem to be crammed full of trivial irritating thoughts which simply won't go away. It can be very difficult to relax and switch off these thoughts and it requires a great deal of effort to do so. Tiredness and irritability may also be signs of anxiety, as is a loss of interest in sexual relations. But the one symptom which is most important for someone with angina is the muscle tension which accompanies anxiety. Chronic tension can result in aches and pains in various parts of the body, and some of these pains, if occurring in the chest or arms, may be interpreted as angina. This can cause the person who experiences these pains to believe they have got very severe heart disease and that they should avoid exercise and cause them to become over-concerned, preoccupied or even obsessed with their condition. This can lead to avoidance of normal activities which maintain good health. Clearly, this vicious circle has to be broken.

Case history

John had thought that he had coped with his heart attack particularly well. But his first angina attack after leaving hospital served to remind him of the ordeal. So he began to take it easy. He very quickly found that he could only walk short distances before experiencing angina. This worried John, and he could feel himself becoming very anxious at the thought of having another angina attack. It very quickly got to the stage where John had begun to think that the next angina attack would be the one that would trigger another heart attack and so he began to do less and less physical activity. It was only after attending the cardiac rehabilitation classes that John realized how out of condition he had allowed himself to become. It took six months for John to realize that it is possible to exercise safely with angina and that providing he stopped when the pains became severe, it would not cause another heart attack.

The anger response

Anger is a strong emotion and all strong emotions can tip the scale of oxygen supply and demand (see Fig 7, page 27) and trigger an angina attack (Verrier *et al*, 1987).[3]

When we feel angry we may only be aware of the bodily sensations which may include an increased heart rate, sweating, stomach churning or nausea. Most people are aware when they feel their 'hackles rising'. However, accompanying these feelings are thoughts which may help to perpetuate the feelings. These thoughts may be ones of 'it's just not fair', 'why me?', 'I look a fool', 'I can't let that person get the better of me', all of which trigger the body to feel more angry. These two are very closely linked and sometimes people will talk of feeling angry as an automatic reaction to a provocation. It is not automatic but it may be happening quickly and the person may be concentrating more on the anger feelings.

Different people behave differently to anger. Some slam doors, shout or hit out, thereby *expressing* it. Some sulk, become withdrawn or sarcastic thereby *suppressing* it. There is no evidence to suggest that either expressing or suppressing anger is better. However, it may be more harmful if you have angina to continually slam doors than it would be to take yourself out of the situation and think before you react.

Case histories

Bill used to shop at the same supermarket each time. One day the cashier made a mistake and short-changed him. Bill's immediate reaction was to think she had done it on purpose because she was stealing money from the till, and he got very angry. He shouted at her and threw the groceries down from the shelf by the checkout. He was asked to leave once his money had been returned. Bill is now unable to walk past that supermarket without remembering the incident, feeling aggrieved and experiencing a mild angina attack. He blames the shop assistant for bringing on his angina.

Sue has been a heavy smoker since senior school. She developed angina symptoms whilst out gardening one day. After many investigations and much worry she was told she had coronary disease and must stop smoking. This she did immediately. When the angina did not go away, Sue began to blame the medical staff for deceiving her into believing it would. She began to experience more angina and eventually underwent a coronary artery bypass operation. This was not completely successful and she remains very angry at the 'incompetent, deceitful medical staff' and also at herself for beginning to smoke in the first place.

The depression response

This is the third response in the triad of emotional reactions. It does not mean those days when we feel a bit low or 'not quite 100 per cent' but it is a more extreme reaction which includes *thoughts, feelings* and *behaviour* which form a pattern of a depressed mood state.

Thoughts: If you feel depressed you may see yourself as useless, incompetent and blameworthy. You may have repetitive trivial thoughts or grossly exaggerate the worst outcome of an event. You may feel your thoughts are sluggish and almost seem to have a will of their own, popping up at the most unlikely times. You may lose interest in things and people or have a general feeling of impending doom for no apparent reason.

Feelings: You may feel frustrated, sad, hopeless and helpless. You may feel unworthy of the attention and help people offer you. An extreme form of depression is when you feel your life is not worth living and you may even make attempts to finish it.

Behaviour: You may appear lethargic, slow, clumsy and may look dopey and sad to outsiders. Sleeplessness is common, with waking up in the early hours and being unable to stimulate any enthusiasm for starting the day. People with angina who respond to stress by becoming depressed may stop exercising and this will lower the amount of exercise you can do before angina occurs. If you are unfit you will have angina at a lower workload and a lower heart rate than someone who is that little bit fitter. The relationship between fitness and angina is explained in greater detail in Chapter 8.

Case history

June was prone to depression when stressed. A number or events in the family got on top of her and she began the characteristic 'wind down'. She lost her job because she couldn't get up in the morning and began staying in bed later and later. She found that the physical effort needed to get the shopping and housework done was just too much and she began having more angina attacks. This upset her and made her feel that the future was hopeless. After some time and help from a psychologist June began to see how her thoughts caused her to behave in ways that made her feel more depressed. By planning more activities she felt she could achieve at, like taking on a new job to pay for help in the home, and by talking over her thoughts and putting them into perspective, she was able to lift her feelings of depression. Breaking into the vicious circle helped her to overcome the depressive aspects of her response to stress.

Behavioural responses to stress

As we can see from Fig 22, an event or trigger can stimulate thoughts which may lead directly to the physical response and ultimately to behaviour. This may happen very quickly as though it were automatic but in fact it goes through the stages outlined in Fig 14 (page 54).

Stress is an extension of arousal. If we are overaroused it is generally experienced as stressful. Some people prefer high levels, some low levels of arousal. It is a question of balancing

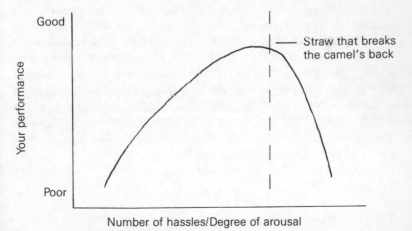

Fig 22: The performance – arousal curve

input (stressful events) with output (your response). Moderate arousal is healthy but overarousal can lead to a poor response. the performance–arousal curve illustrates this.

The point at which we go over the top of the curve is the point at which our body tells us we are stressed. Again how we respond will differ: some people will resort to smoking excessively, some turn to alcohol, some take on more work or more exercise, some stop exercising and some simply flop in front of the television each evening, exhausted from the day. Research has shown that people who are stressed have more problems in taking decisions and carrying out routine tasks. Entering a room and forgetting why you went there is a typical example. This is called a *cognitive error* and can be quite amusing unless you are an airline pilot or nuclear energy plant engineer!

Case history

Colin was proud of his ability to perform his job in an engineering firm. Very rapidly, through sheer hard work, he rose up through the ranks to become chief engineer. His family began to notice signs of stress but Colin denied this. He was smoking very heavily and finished work by going to the pub each night. His relationship with his wife and children began to deteriorate as he spent more time at work and less at home. Even when he was home he seemed to be working or organizing the fishing club of which he was secretary. Colin began to have twinges of pain in his chest after finding himself in his car in a part of town he had never visited and not knowing how he got there. He ignored the episode. His job suffered, he caused a number of small accidents by making 'stupid errors'. One day it all came to a head. Colin had left a vital piece of machinery on and this ruined a major job that had taken six months to produce. He suffered his worst ever angina attack and was taken to hospital with a suspected heart attack. He was relieved when the diagnosis was not a heart attack. Colin was feeling quite well a few days later and ready to return to work when his boss unexpectedly visited him in hospital to tell him he had been replaced due to his series of costly errors over the last six months. Looking back over the past few months he very much regretted not taking notice of his early warning signs.

The thoughts response

What you think affects how you feel and behave. Under stress people have been shown to distort and exaggerate events which may not warrant it and this can lead to more stress. You may be more ready to 'jump to conclusions' and form inaccurate impressions about circumstances. These irrational thoughts are called *cognitive distortions*. When these cognitive distortions occur they can fuel your typical emotional response which may be anxiety, anger or depression and cause you to react in an extreme way – just like Bill at the supermarket (page 103). These cognitive distortions may be very difficult to pinpoint, because we are not always aware of our thoughts. However, this is a skill which you can learn and with practice you can tune into your stressful thoughts. Once you have identified them you can examine them in a calm light. Many of these thoughts appear to be automatic and uncontrollable. But the art of examining them makes them controllable. It is helpful first to simply be able to identify *your* particular thoughts and responses.

Joe woke up one morning to find his car had been stolen, his initial reaction was to think 'how could I be so stupid as not to put it in the garage? How will I get to work? My boss will be furious, I was late yesterday too! He will blame me. Perhaps I'll go sick. I do feel sick, oh no! I'm having an angina attack. I can't cope with all this and my angina. This attack doesn't feel like the others, oh! my goodness it's not, it's a heart attack!'

Mary woke up to the same event and thought 'Oh no! This will cause me some hassle. Wait a minute though, don't let's get carried away here. Do I need the car today? Yes, well okay, stay calm and think about it. It is fully insured so there is no problem, I am also covered for car hire in these circumstances so I'll do that. Well, it could be worse I suppose. Anyway, I'll cope, it's an excuse to have that half day off I've been promising myself.'

Thoughts are powerful triggers to booster further stress responses. Because Joe overreacted he triggered a severe angina attack where Mary was able to short-circuit her stress response by keeping her thoughts calm and rational.

Long-term responses to stress

We have covered the main physiological, emotional, cognitive and behavioural responses to stress. You will be able to identify one or more responses that you have experienced at some time.

These are all *normal* responses to stress on a continuum from mild to extreme. Someone who responded minimally to stress at one time may respond in an extreme way at a different time. The short-term mild responses may not be harmful at all but the long-term chronic stress responses can be catastrophic for some people.

We are all genetically programmed to develop certain illnesses under certain conditions favourable for that illness. What we don't know is *what* illnesses, under *which* conditions, and for *whom*. Stress may act as a trigger for one or other of those illnesses, causing the body to identify its weak system and respond accordingly by showing signs of an illness. But because the symptoms of these illnesses may cause stress responses in themselves it is very difficult to know which came first, the stress or the illness.

There is sound research evidence to suggest that the way we behave (and therefore think and feel) can trigger coronary disease including hypertension, chronic pain (Leavitt *et al*, 1979),[4] digestive ulcers and bowel disorders (Whitehead and Schusten, 1985).[5] There is some, albeit weak, evidence to suggest that stress may also be related to asthma, rheumatoid arthritis and diabetes. This does not always imply that stress *causes* these diseases but we know that for some people stressful events can trigger an exacerbation or 'flare-up' of the illness. This is especially true in angina. Chronic stress can manifest itself as chronic back pain, headaches, unexplained fatigue in one's limbs, undue disability from a physical illness, sexual problems and many other disorders.

Being labelled 'ill' or 'disabled' can have detrimental effects on the way some people behave. Being told you have a chronic illness can have an effect on the way you think and feel about yourself also. For example, if someone has a mental picture of a person with a long-term illness as a passive, pathetic figure who cannot perform essential tasks, then this will cause them to lose respect for themselves and to see themselves as dependent and even a burden on others. This can lead to severely strained relationships within the family. They may also believe that having a chronic illness (such as angina) means they have to stop doing any physical work and retire to the armchair. By behaving in this excessively passive way (known as *sick role behaviour*) they let their fitness lapse, bringing on more angina and other aches and pains as the joints and muscles deteriorate from underuse. This may begin the downward spiral of sadness, debilitation and depression.

There is good research evidence to suggest that people may be more disabled by their thoughts and feelings about their illness and what it means to them than the actual extent of the illness warrants.

People who behave, think and feel in this way have very poor expectations from life. They often feel they are not worthy of help and successfully merge into becoming the disabled person they had the image of in their mind. Sometimes they become irritable through frustration and may be aggressive to others. Because they behave in this way they may isolate themselves from their family and friends and eventually find themselves receiving little support from others and become more dependent on strangers for assistance.

This behaviour can have an effect on the way others see the person too. The medical and social services often treat disabled people as passive, pathetic recipients who will accept any standards of care. This is not too surprising if this is how the person behaves and thinks of him/herself. So, once again a vicious circle is set up with people being more disabled than their physical condition necessitates because their thoughts, behaviour and feelings play a role in their 'disability'.

Tom used to be the life and soul of the party. He was a keen fisherman and everyone who knew him enjoyed his company. When he was told he had angina Tom remembered how a good friend of his had died from a heart attack and he connected the two. He began to 'take it easy'. He retired from work, gave up fishing, and things went from bad to worse. He became irritable and frustrated because he could not do what he used to do and because he missed the social contact with friends.

Arguments with his wife increased because, as she said, 'He's around the house, getting in the way, all day long'. He began to see himself as a burden and lost respect for himself. He became snappy to the grandchildren and eventually they stopped visiting.

After a year Tom had an angiogram which showed he had very mild coronary disease and he enrolled in the physical training classes. Slowly but surely he regained some physical fitness and the angina became less troublesome. He began to renew his friendships and took up fishing again.

Tom still cannot do all the things he would like to do but now

he accepts it. He still believes he is a person to be respected and
his friends and family enjoy the new, more relaxed Tom as much
as the one before he had angina.

Now that we have covered most of the stress responses, fill in
your answers to the stress questionnaire which follows and try
to build up a picture of your predominant responses to stress.
Knowing yourself is half the battle of changing. The next chapter
will look in more detail at ways of controlling your stress
responses.

Stress Questionnaire

Answer
Yes / No

+   1. Is your appetite at the moment poorer
       than usual?
o   2. Do you feel tired often?
★   3. Do you drink too much?
o   4. Do your family tell you you fuss too
       much?
+   5. Do you suffer from odd aches, pains or
       muscle tension?
o   6. Are you inclined to think the worst of
       people?
o   7. Do you worry about a large number of
       things?
★   8. Do you feel restless for no good reason?
o   9. Do you find yourself making 'silly'
       mistakes often?
+ 10. Do you suffer from frequent headaches?
o 11. Do people you know say you jump to
       conclusions too quickly?
★ 12. Is your temper short?
+ 13. Do you suffer from blurred vision or
       ringing in your ears?
★ 14. Are you indecisive?
+ 15. Is your sexual appetite good?
o 16. Are you a gloomy person?
+ 17. Do you smoke too much?

o 18. Do you feel sad or low for no apparent reason?

+ 19. Do you ever feel shaky or have muscle twitches?

o 20. Is your head ever filled with monotonous, repetitive thoughts?

+ 21. Do you suffer from breathlessness?

o 22. Do you feel hopeless or helpless?

o 23. Do you ever feel like you simply can't cope any more?

+ 24. Do you suffer from indigestion, flatulence or nausea?

o 25. Are your relationships at work bad?

★ 26. Is your concentration poor?

o 27. Do you feel incompetent at most things?

+ 28. Are you ever aware of your heart racing or pounding?

+ 29. Do you ever get chest pain?

★ 30. Do you eat rapidly?

★ 31. Do you miss routine appointments with the dentist or doctor frequently?

o 32. Have you woken up worrying about things in the last month?

+ 33. Do you have backache often?

+ 34. Do you sweat a lot or flush a lot?

o 35. Do you feel angry or frustrated with people often?

o 36. Do you feel irritable for no good reason?

★ 37. Are your relationships at home poor?

★ 38. Do you sigh or yawn a lot?

+ 39. Do you have high blood pressure?

★ 40. Is it difficult to get out of bed every morning?

Scoring key

+ = physical responses
○ = emotional–thought responses
★ = behavioural responses

Give yourself one point for each 'yes' answer.

If you answered 'yes' to predominantly ★ questions, you usually respond to stress in a behavioural way, that is, your behaviour, the things you do, indicate to yourself and others that you are feeling stressed.

If you answered 'yes' to questions marked + mainly, then your predominant reaction to stress is a physical one. This means you feel your body becoming upset when things get too much.

If you answered 'yes' to ○ marked questions more than the other two, you tend to respond to stress by becoming overemotional (angry, anxious or depressed).

However, if you answer about 15 points with an even mixture of all three ★,○,+, you don't have a predominant response but you experience stress in all these ways.

Anything below 15 points means you are not especially stressed at the moment.

CHAPTER 7

Stress and angina: relaxation skills

Chapter 6 has described the symptoms of stress and in particular how our body responds to acute (sudden) and chronic (long-term) stress. This chapter concentrates on the opposite response to stress, the *relaxation response*. It is the natural antidote to stress. Because no one method will suit everyone, this chapter provides you with four main types of relaxation training to enable you to choose one which best fits in with your lifestyle.

Just as stress can become a way of life if it goes on for long enough, so too can relaxation. Relaxation training has to be learned over time and most importantly it has to be practised before it can be learned. Just like learning any other skill, playing the piano, typewriting or learning to drive, the more practice you put in, the more expert you will become.

How well you relax does not mean how often you flop in front of the television after a day's work, or whether you sleep eight hours per night. It is better measured by the mixture of physical and mental activities you do which enable you to switch off from the routine worries of the day. Some people find sport relaxing and even vigorous activity such as running or squash can clear one's mind. Other people find doing jigsaw puzzles, playing bridge or chess just as relaxing. The secret of being able to relax fully is to have a balance of activities, both mental and physical, which occupy your thoughts. So, relaxation is an *activity*, both mental and physical, *not* a semi-comatose state which finds you nodding off to sleep.

Why do we need relaxation?

The benefits of relaxation have been acknowledged for centuries in the Eastern world but the West has taken a very long time waking up to them. Researchers, such as Benson at Harvard University in the USA,[1] have clearly established a number of effects which are due to relaxation. These benefits have been seen in people who have clinical problems such as anxiety and in others without problems.

Firstly, whilst relaxation techniques are being used to treat people with these hyper-arousal problems, more people are beginning to realize that everyone can benefit from some form of relaxation training. Secondly, there is now a great deal of interest shown in treating people with physical disorders using some form of relaxation. The evidence that relaxation can help in the treatment of high blood pressure, coronary heart disease, bowel disorders, asthma and angina is now strong. Some doctors assert that relaxation training should be the treatment of choice, not just the last resort, in some physical disease.[1]

Deep relaxation has a number of physiological and psychological effects. It can slow breathing and promote deep breathing which has the effect of decreasing the amount of oxygen the body needs to 'tick over'. It promotes the more efficient use of the oxygen it receives so the heart is able to work harder with slightly less oxygen. This relaxing effect on the heart makes it able to rest slightly and therefore decrease the amount of blood it has to push through. It decreases the oxygen demand of the heart.

There is some evidence that relaxation, especially prolonged relaxation, can decrease the cholesterol (fatty substances) in the blood. It may also promote tissue repairing and healing.[2] Research on relaxation training in patients after major surgery has shown that their wounds heal more quickly than those who did not learn to relax. Whilst some of these effects are produced by sleep, they are not seen till about three-quarters of the way through a night's sleep, so relaxation appears to bring some of the benefits of sleep in a shorter time.

The benefits of relaxation on psychological functioning are also well documented. People who practise relaxation are said to be more confident, have a more positive frame of mind, have high self-esteem and a better sense of humour due to relaxation training than people who do not practise relaxation. These same people are reported as having more energy and also get less fatigued.

There is no doubt that learning to relax by whichever method suits you best is a positive way of contributing to your overall good health. The exercises in this chapter are available on a tape (see further resources).

Are there side-effects of relaxation?

In people without psychological or psychiatric problems who want to learn how to relax there are no known side-effects. Although some people say they do not enjoy the feeling of detachment that some forms of relaxation can bring, with careful preparation by the relaxation teacher these unpleasant feelings should go. Some people, again a very small minority, complain of lightheadedness, hunger or tiredness after relaxation. This probably occurs because the body has a chance to rest and only 'tick over' rather than running at its usual speed and these sensations feel strange because your attention is sharply brought to them. They can easily be overcome by not relaxing when you are tired or hungry (or immediately after a heavy meal). Also, when you end your relaxation exercise you should do so slowly, and not rush back into a hectic pace of life for 10 to 15 minutes after relaxing.

Deep breathing

The importance of deep breathing in relaxation cannot be overstated. Although breathing occurs without conscious thought, it can be controlled by conscious means. Because it is involuntary, the way we breathe can reflect our state of relaxation. For example, without being aware of it anxious people will breathe shallowly and rapidly, using only the upper part of their chest. If they are very anxious they may sigh frequently as do people who are depressed.

There are three main types of breathing, thoracic (chest), costal (very rapid panting) and abdominal (stomach) breathing. In everyday life we most often use the thoracic type. This fills the top third of our lungs with air each time we take a breath. When asked to take a deep breath most people would expand their chest pulling in their abdomen, this is not the correct type of deep breathing needed for relaxation. A proper full breath starts in the abdomen pushing it out slowly and the chest only expands slightly. This way the bottom two-thirds of the lungs are filled with air also.

What are the effects of deep breathing?

The main effect is to induce relaxation. It does this by filling the lungs fully with oxygen and pushing carbon dioxide, the waste product of breathing, out of the lungs. The extra amount of oxygen is carried to the brain, and can cause the pleasant euphoric effects of relaxation.

Where to practise deep breathing

The main benefit of deep breathing is that it can be done anywhere at any time. Some people find it easier to do sitting in a chair than lying down where it is difficult to see what your abdomen is doing.

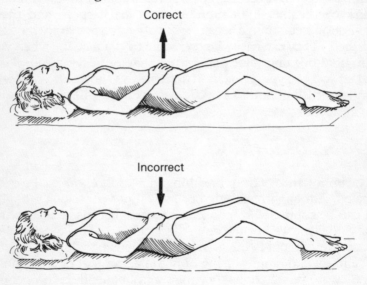

Fig 23: Deep breathing exercises

How to deep breathe

Step 1
It is always better to begin learning any relaxation skills by lying down in a warm, comfortable place where you will not be disturbed.

Step 2
Begin by thinking slow, relaxing thoughts. When you have found a comfortable position place your right hand over your

upper abdomen about the level of your navel and your left hand over your chest.

Step 3

Begin the breath in and count slowly for five seconds. You can pace this by counting '1,000, 2,000, 3,000, 4,000, 5,000'. You should feel your right hand rise and your left hand staying in about the same position. It is helpful to imagine you have a balloon of air under your right hand which is gradually filling with air as you breathe in. When you have reached '5,000' you will be at the top of your breath; don't pause here, just let the air escape from your lungs at the same pace you counted it in. So, count down from 5,000 . . . to 1,000, slowly letting your lungs expel the air in them. Begin by doing this for three to four times and then breathe normally. It is important not to do this more frequently than that because you may begin to feel lightheaded or dizzy as too much oxygen gets to your brain in one go. This is not dangerous but it can be unpleasant. After a break of five to ten minutes you can begin again but don't do more than three rounds of five deep breaths at one go.

Once you have learned this simple technique you can use it to prepare yourself for relaxation any time, anywhere.

Progressive muscular relaxation

After activity, or when you are anxious, your muscles contract and become tense, but you may not be aware of this. Unless you actively release this tension this can build up and become chronic. Chronic tension has three main effects:
a) it causes discomfort in the muscles
b) it exposes the muscles and surrounding structures – ligaments and bones – to physical stress and potential injury
c) it can act as a cue for anxiety.

Progressive muscular relaxation works in three ways. Firstly, it teaches you the difference between the sensation of tension and the sensation of relaxation in the muscles. Secondly, it breaks into the cue for anxiety. Thirdly, the muscles become more relaxed if tensed then relaxed rather than simply 'let go' from a resting position.

The whole procedure will take about 15 to 20 minutes. It is not possible, especially in the beginning, to cut down this time. When learning this skill it is essential to practise at least once a day, preferably twice. When it has been fully learned it may be possible to 'top up' less often but at this stage, the more you practise the more benefits you will feel.

Where you practise is also very important. You will need a quiet, darkened room where you are sure you won't be disturbed. It is not ideal to practise in the bedroom as there will be associations with sleeping there. As you should be alert but relaxed, not drowsy, at the end of the exercise it is better to avoid places associated with sleep. But if it is the only room available, make sure you do not try to practise when you are tired. You should also avoid deep relaxation after a heavy meal as your digestion may be distracting and you may fall asleep. If there is a telephone in the room, take it off the receiver – put a 'do not disturb' notice on the door if necessary. It is also important to ensure the room is warm, as when you relax your body temperature drops which can make you more sensitive to a cold room. Close the curtains so that you can focus all your attention on your bodily sensations.

Step 1
Lie on your back on a firm surface with your head, neck and back well supported. Remove your shoes, belt, tie, contact lenses or spectacles and loosen any restrictive clothing. Allow your ankles to flop apart, keep your knees together and lay your arms beside your body with the palms turned uppermost. Close your eyes.

Step 2
Begin by thinking slow, relaxing thoughts. Bring to mind any comfortable relaxing feeling you can remember. This may be a day on the beach, lying on a hill in the sun, or anything you have found relaxing in the past. Take three slow deep breaths, just like you have learned in the deep breathing section. Do not rush through this section, as mental preparation is as important as the physical procedure.

Step 3
When you are ready begin to focus your attention on your body and feel the support from the structure you are lying on, bring all your attention to your feet, toes and ankles. Tense them by pushing the toes away from your body, hold the tension for

about five seconds and then relax. Slowly let all of the tension fade away.

Then bring your attention to your lower limbs. Again tense the calf muscles by pushing your heels down away from your body, hold, then relax. Also, bring your toes up in the other direction. This will fully stretch your calf muscles, hold, then relax. Moving up to your thighs, tense them whilst leaving the lower limbs relaxed, hold, and relax. Notice the difference between tension and relaxation, concentrate on the sensation. Next, raise your legs about six inches away from the bed, hold, and then relax. You can omit this last exercise if you have a back problem.

Now moving up to the buttocks, clench them together, raising your pelvis off the bed slightly, hold, then relax. Make sure you pause between the muscle groups to appreciate the difference between tension and relaxation. Concentrate your attention now on your lower back. Repeat the tension by arching your back, only slightly, and slowly letting it sink back down into the bed or floor.

Moving up to your arms, making a fist with both hands, tense your hands and forearms, hold, then relax. Move up to your biceps, tense these by bending your arms at the elbow and bringing your fist up to your shoulder, again hold, then relax.

Letting your hands spread out comfortably, bring your attention to the sensation of relaxation in the whole of your body from your chest downwards.

Now concentrate on your shoulders, shrugging them up to your ears, tensing all of your upper back, neck and shoulders, then relax. Slowly rotate your head around to your left shoulder whilst keeping it on the floor or the bed. Feel the tension in the right side of your neck, hold, then relax. Repeat that exercise on the opposite side. Now bring your chin towards your chest, tensing the muscles in the back of your neck, hold the tension, then relax. Push your head back down onto the pillow, raising your chin to the ceiling, hold, then relax.

Now focus on the muscles of your jaw, eyes, forehead, scalp and tongue. First clench your jaw tight, holding the tension in your lower and upper jaw, and then relax. Press your tongue hard into the roof of your mouth with your mouth closed, hold the tension and then relax. Now screw up your eyes as if you have soap in them, hold, and relax. Make a frown across your forehead, knitting your eyebrows together, feel the tension across your forehead, hold, and then relax. Enjoy this sensation of warmth and comfort which comes into the whole of your face and head when you relax.

Enjoy this feeling for a few moments. Then mentally check through all of the muscles you have relaxed to see if there is any tension left. If there is, repeat the exercise for that muscle group.

Step 4

Once you have lain enjoying the feeling of relaxation for some minutes, begin to bring your attention back to your surroundings. Take a deep breath, feel the air entering your lungs bringing new fresh vigour, stretch your limbs, toes, fingers and open your eyes. You will feel new life entering your body and a new feeling of deep relaxation and mental alertness. If you have followed this procedure carefully you should be looking forward to the next practice. However, we all learn at a different pace and do not be disheartened if you did not get the full benefit this time. It will get better with practice.

Cue-controlled relaxation

The aim of this method of relaxation is to pair the deep breathing with the progressive muscular relaxation so that the deep breath acts as a trigger or cue to relax. Before practising this method,

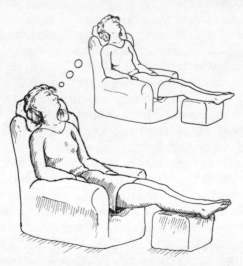

Fig 24: Cue-controlled relaxation

it is best to become familiar with both deep breathing and progressive muscular relaxation first.

Once you are skilled at the progressive technique, you will be able to cue your body to relax by taking a deep breath and switching on the relaxation wherever you are. This will take time and effort to learn and will not happen at once.

Step 1. Begin by getting comfortable and preparing as though for the progressive muscular technique.

Step 2. Settle your mind, and bring into your conscious attention the relaxing scene you have been focusing on in the progressive technique. Whilst in this stage of relaxation, choose a word or phrase which seems to sum up the feelings you have of relaxation. For some people this may be 'peace' or 'warm glow' or 'relax', anything which can become your personal trigger.

Step 3. Begin by focusing on the lower half of your body just as you did for the progressive technique, but this time as you tense those muscles in turn begin the tension with a deep breath in. Remember to breathe from your abdomen and not from your chest only. As you get to the top of your breath you should be at the peak of the tension in the muscle group you are tensing. When you have reached this point begin the slow breath out, releasing that tension and mentally saying your cue word – 'RE-LAX' – or whatever you have chosen.

Continue working up your body, through the different muscle groups, tensing and breathing in, relaxing and breathing out. Do not forget to use your cue word. In between each group of muscles being tensed, it is important to breathe normally and slowly, do not continue to deep breathe in between. The aim is to pair the breathing with the action of relaxing so that in future a single deep breath, or even your special word, will trigger the relaxation response.

Step 4. Once you have worked through the major muscle groups, and this should take you about 20 minutes, you can enjoy the feeling of relaxation for a few minutes and then begin to come out of the relaxation. Follow the instructions of Step 4 of the progressive relaxation. You should finish feeling relaxed and calm, alert and invigorated.

It is important to practise cue-controlled relaxation regularly. About once to twice daily is ideal. Try to vary the times at which you do the practice and make a note of the effect that was achieved. This way you will begin to learn what time of day suits you best.

Rapid relaxation

The techniques of relaxation described so far have all required preparation and special conditions; a quiet, warm room, 20 minutes or so of time, and a private place. The advantage of rapid relaxation is that it does not require any of these preconditions. It will only take about two minutes to practise and can be done anywhere. However, it is not possible to bypass the other techniques, going straight to rapid relaxation and expect it to have enormous effects. You will only achieve the full benefit from

Fig 25: Rapid relaxation

rapid relaxation by first practising deep breathing, progressive muscular and cue-controlled relaxation. Rapid relaxation is a type of shorthand version of the full relaxation, but like shorthand you cannot use it unless you have learned to read and write first. Once you have learned this technique, however, you can use it any time and to the exclusion of the others if you so wish.

Step 1. Begin by reminding yourself of the word you use to cue the relaxation response. Stand up straight, with your feet about six inches apart and your arms hanging loosely by your sides. Close your eyes and focus your attention on your bodily sensations. Become aware of where your limbs are in space and feel the ground beneath your feet. In particular, become aware of your right arm, hand and shoulder, this is the one group of muscles into which you will put all of the tension in your body.

Step 2. Begin by taking a slow deep breath, as before, and as you do so build the tension first in your fingers, clenching your fist, then in your forearm, elbow joint, biceps and shoulder. Keep your arm rigid, straight and close to your side. The peak of the tension should be reached when you have reached the top of your breath. Mentally say your cue word. Gradually let out the breath and the tension, pacing them together and matching the rhythm of the breath in. Imagine all of the tension dripping out of your hand and fingers as you stand relaxed and calm. It is very important to keep the rest of your body relaxed whilst you are focusing all of the tension in your right arm.

Step 3. Repeat Step 2 if you need to, but make sure you are not rushing through either the mental preparation, the deep breath in or out or the physical tensing. Stand and enjoy the feeling of complete relaxation for a few moments.

Step 4. Bring your focus back to your surroundings, take a deep breath in to invigorate you and shake your limbs loose for a few seconds.

This exercise has the great advantage of being usable whilst going about your normal activities. For example, while shopping you could stand and pretend to look in a shop window, or in an argument you could excuse yourself and go to the bathroom and return more in control, or immediately prior to exercise, say at the bottom of a hill. More about preparation for exercise at the end of the chapter.

Self-hypnosis

The term 'hypnosis' conjures up images of people in zombie-like states, performing childlike, often degrading acts against their will. Whilst this may happen in show performances, this is not what you will be expected to learn in this book. Because hypnosis has had such a bad press people are either reluctant to use it and may be frightened of it or they may expect it to perform miracles. Some of the myths about it will be examined in this section.

Myth No. 1. You have to be a 'certain type' of person to be hypnotized

Not true. People are certainly different in the degree to which they respond to hypnotic suggestions but it is not only one type of person who will respond. Suggestibility can be measured and a good hypnotherapist would test your powers of self-suggestion before teaching hypnosis. Suggestibility is not related to gullibility, or intelligence, or your sex, or any of the other misconceptions you may have heard. It is correlated with a good imagination and people differ in the degree to which they can imagine things in their mind's eye.

Myth No. 2. Hypnotists are in control of your mind

Not true. All hypnosis is self-hypnosis, or *self-suggestion*, and you are at all times in control of what you are doing. When participants in stage shows of hypnosis do ridiculous things, they are simply going along with suggestions the hypnotist has made. If the hypnotist made a suggestion that the participant did not want to comply with, they simply would not do it.

Myth No. 3. You may be stuck in a trance

Not true. Whilst it is agreed that suggestions can be very powerful and the hypnotic state can be very deep, if there was danger of any sort present the respondent would come out of the state. Hypnosis will not reduce you to a zombie. People often drift into sleep under hypnosis then sleep and wake up quite normally.

Myth No. 4. When you are in a trance you don't know what's happening

Not true. You may be less aware of some events going on around you at first but generally as you become more practised your senses sharpen. The hypnotic state may be so pleasant and relaxing that you choose not to accept some sounds or sights around you. But at the first sign of danger you would respond as though you were fully awake. Hypnosis is an altered, intensified state of consciousness which most users of hypnosis find stimulating and deeply relaxing.

Myth No. 5. You cannot hypnotize yourself

Not true. You will be taught how to induce the state of hypnosis yourself. All hypnosis is listening to your mind making suggestions and your body going along with those suggestions. It may help to have someone make the suggestions for you, but it is not essential.

Listening to your own suggestions

Before launching into self-hypnosis it helps to train your mind to focus on your suggestions and this can be done by learning *passive relaxation*. It is called passive because it does not involve tensing the muscle groups but relies on your ability to induce relaxation by your thoughts alone.

Step 1. Begin as you would for the active, progressive relaxation technique. Place yourself in a comfortable, warm, private place.

Step 2. Bring your attention to your body and its sensations and try to shut out the sounds around you. Close your eyes. Begin by doing a couple of deep breaths.

Step 3. Imagine that you are lying in a secluded position in the warmth of the sun. You may choose your garden at home, a beach or a hill top somewhere. The place doesn't matter but it should be one that you can see with your mind's eye. Concentrate on the sounds, sights, smells or tastes you would experience in this place.

Now imagine the sun bathing your body with warmth. Begin by feeling it over your toes and feet, up over your shins, calves, knees and thighs, over your lower abdomen, hands, forearms, upper arms, chest, shoulders, neck and face. Try slowly to let this warmth caress your body and as you feel the warmth also feel the sensation of lightness in your body. Feel your body becoming free and light, almost lifting off the ground. Imagine you are floating on a cushion of air between you and the ground.

Try to conjure up the sights you would see, the sounds, perhaps of the birds or waves, the smells of the grass or salt air and even the colours of the sky, the grass, the sand. Keep the scene as vivid in your mind as you can and just enjoy the feeling of being relaxed by your mind and body.

Step 4. After a couple of minutes begin to bring your attention back to the room you are in, take one or two deep breaths and come back to feeling fully alert and refreshed.

This exercise, if practised, will prepare you for self-hypnosis.

How to carry out self-hypnosis

Step 1. Begin this exercise as you would any of the others. Find a quiet, warm, comfortable room where you won't be disturbed. You can do this exercise lying or sitting. It may be best to learn it by using your usual relaxation posture.

Step 2. Pick a spot on the wall or ceiling which is almost out of your field of vision, so that you have to strain to see it. Fix your eyes on that spot and in doing so fix your concentration. Begin by taking five deep breaths, slowly and deeply, as you have learned before. With each breath feel your body become more relaxed, also feel the strain on your eyes as you hold your gaze on that spot. When you get to the third breath feel your eyes flicker, blink and water. At five close your eyes and use this as a cue to quickly bring on the deep relaxation. Take a further deep breath as you focus on the sensation of body relaxation.

Now imagine that you are at the top of five steps. You will take five further deep breaths and with each one imagine yourself descending one of the steps. Take this slowly and feel the sensation of greater relaxation with each step down.

Picture yourself approaching a lakeside. Take, in your mind, 20 steps towards the lake. As you do so, imagine the number turning over in your mind and with each one feel yourself become more relaxed. At 20 you will have reached the waterside. Gaze at the water and imagine the ripples caressing your body and taking your troubles away. Just enjoy this feeling of carefreeness and deep relaxation. As you do this the next step will be to learn how to bring yourself out of this state and very quickly back into it.

Step 3. Pick a colour or sight that you can see in this lakeside scene or use your cue word and concentrate on it for a few seconds. Feel as fully relaxed as you are able, for as long as you wish. Think of a word that sums up how you feel. It may be your cue word. This word will become your cue to be as relaxed as you are now, when you use it at other times. (That is called a *post-hypnotic suggestion*.)

You can also suggest to yourself how relaxed and comfortable and vigorous you would like to feel in situations where you often experience angina. You will also find you will learn to relax more quickly if you can suggest to yourself, while under self-hypnosis, that you will feel more relaxed, more deeply, more easily, each time you practise these exercises. Then begin to wake yourself up gently and slowly. Take three deep breaths and as you do so count yourself from 'five' to 'one'. With each number feel yourself become more alert and relaxed. Once you reach 'one' let your eyes open and stretch your limbs.

Step 4. If you choose to, you can go even deeper, more quickly, by fixing your eyes on that same spot as before. Take those same five deep breaths and as you do so feel your eyes ache and flicker. Feel your eyelids get heavier and at the fifth breath let them close. Enjoy the feeling of relaxation as it caresses your body with warmth and lightness. Take yourself back to your scene, staying for a few moments.

Step 5. Finally, bring your attention back to your surroundings. Take a couple of deep breaths, feel your lungs expand with the cool invigorating air and notice how much sharper your concentration is, how alert you have become.

This exercise is just one way of using your own suggestions to help yourself achieve relaxation. Practise as often as you can. The more you practise the more expert you will become.

Angina, relaxation and exercise

Gradual exercise can strengthen your heart muscle like any other muscle and is therefore essential in helping you to manage angina. Once your muscle is strong it will require less oxygen to beat and will be able to respond to extra demands better. When you are emotionally aroused this places an unwanted strain on the heart muscle. (This is discussed in more detail in Chapter 1.) You can reduce this strain by being fully relaxed before doing any exercise.

Prepare for exercise, say going for a walk, by deciding how far you are able to go before becoming breathless or having angina. This point is predictable for most people, for example, from your front door to the post box. This is your *exertion point*.

Stage 1. Decide where this exertion point is and plan to walk to a point just short of it, perhaps the door before the green one. This is your *sub-exertion point*. Begin by thinking positively 'I will reach the sub-exertion point without pain'.

Stage 2. Use any of the methods of relaxation you have been taught. Imagine in your mind's eye getting to the exertion point, remaining calm and feeling relaxed and comfortable.

Stage 3. Start walking slowly towards this point. Take a couple of deep breaths, focus on your breathing and how well you feel. When you reach the sub-exertion point, take another deep breath and then carry on. All the time focus your attention on the breathing and how well you feel.

Stage 4. Evaluate how well you did. When you are able to achieve this exertion point comfortably then set the next target a little way ahead and proceed in the same way.

Remember your exertion point may be influenced by how well you are feeling or the weather or many other factors. Do not move your exertion point on a day when you are not feeling 100 per cent well. Just practise at the previous level. When you feel well set your target a little higher.

This form of preparation can be used for any type of exercise from spectator sports to swimming. You can never over-relax!

Keeping a relaxation diary

When learning a new skill it is very useful to keep a diary of your progress as athletes do. It can provide you with valuable information on where, when and how you are best able to relax. Sometimes a pattern emerges which indicates the best time of day for you. If you are constantly falling asleep on the evening session, for example, then change your time for relaxation. Fill in each record immediately after the session when the feelings are still fresh in your mind (see Fig 26).

Summary

This chapter has been about relaxation training. There are two important points to remember.

1. Just as we all react differently to stress, we each have different ways of relaxing, so choose the one which suits you best.
2. Relaxation is a skill just like playing a musical instrument or sailing a boat: it requires frequent practice to gain expertise and pleasure from it.

If you would like more information on relaxation training, Yoga training, meditation training or self-hypnosis it is likely that

DATE	TIME	WHERE?	RESULT/ EFFECT

Fig 26: Relaxation practise

classes that are run in your area will be advertised in the local press. However, if they are not, you may try contacting the local psychology service in your area who may give you the name of an approved practitioner. Or contact the British Society for Experimental and Clinical Hypnosis who will hold a list of approved practitioners of hypnotherapy.

CHAPTER 8

Angina and exercise

It would appear from the many articles in the media in the last decade or so as though exercise had just been invented. Somehow, whenever one mentions exercise, pictures of exhausted sweating bodies leaping about in leotards or tracksuits readily spring to mind. It need not be like that. In its broadest form, every time we walk somewhere or go upstairs or do some housework we are exercising. It is an unavoidable part of everyday life. However, to a person with angina exercise is often the cause of their discomfort and understandably, therefore, regarded with apprehension or fear.

This chapter will dispel some of the mystique and hype surrounding exercise and explain how you can benefit by doing just a *little* more activity than you do at present. It will also explain how exercise can be safe and fun.

We all know that when we exert ourselves our heart rate, that is, the number of heartbeats per minute, increases. We also know that this increase in heart rate is responsible for triggering angina as described in Chapter 1. But why does the heart rate increase with exercise?

Basic physiology of exercise

Any form of exercise involves work done by muscles. Muscles contain fibres which contract or shorten when they receive messages from the brain via the nerves. In the same way that a car engine requires fuel to make it work, so do the muscles. The fuel that muscles 'run' on is mainly glucose but with considerable exercise the body can break down fat and use that as fuel. In order for the energy to be released from the fuel, the body needs oxygen.

When we breathe, oxygen is drawn into the lungs. Blood in the blood vessels of the lungs absorbs the oxygen and then travels back to the heart to be pumped round the body. As the blood passes through the tissues of the body it releases oxygen where it is needed, for example working muscles. Blood flows round the body continuously, releasing oxygen and absorbing carbon dioxide which is a waste product – like the exhaust from a car engine. Carbon dioxide is then passed from the blood when it returns to the lungs to pick up more oxygen. The carbon dioxide is then breathed out by the lungs.

Muscle activity in the presence of enough oxygen is called *aerobic exercise*. But if the body is overworked, the blood supply cannot deliver enough oxygen to the muscles. The muscles will continue to work for a while with less oxygen, but in doing so, make a product called lactic acid. Lactic acid collects in the muscle making it stiff and painful, and ultimately the muscle stops working. Muscle activity without enough oxygen is called *anaerobic exercise*.

To summarize, in order for our muscles to work efficiently they need oxygen, which is provided by the lungs. The oxygen is carried to the muscles by the blood which is pumped round the body by the heart.

The reason that your heart rate increases with exercise is to meet the demands for more oxygen. The harder the exercise, the more oxygen the muscles require. The more oxygen the muscles need, the faster the blood must be pumped round the body by the heart. The lungs respond to the increased demand for oxygen by breathing more deeply and more quickly, and the heart responds by contracting more quickly and powerfully. This is why the heart rate, the number of heartbeats per minute, increases during exercise.

The heart itself contains muscle and, like the skeletal muscles in the limbs, it too needs a constant supply of oxygen in order for it to function. Like skeletal muscle, the harder the heart muscle has to work, the more oxygen it requires. If the heart is pumping quickly to increase the circulation and oxygen supply to the working muscles in the body, but because of narrowing of the coronary arteries (see Chapter 1) its own needs for increased oxygen are not being met, the result is pain. This explains why angina is felt during exercise.

What is fitness?

Fitness is your *functional capacity*, that is your capacity to perform physical work. The amount of physical work you can do is dependent upon the amount of oxygen received and used by the body. The more it can use, the more work you can do. But, the more work you do, the more oxygen your body needs! The greatest amount of oxygen a person can use during physical work is termed *maximal oxygen uptake*. Physiologists define functional capacity in terms of oxygen consumption, so a person's maximal functional capacity or fitness is measured by their maximal oxygen uptake. For example, the maximal oxygen uptake of a top athlete such as a marathon runner is roughly twice as high as that of an average person.

A person's fitness or functional capacity is assessed by exercise tests on a treadmill or bicycle ergometer (see Chapter 2).

How is fitness affected by angina?

The body's fitness is determined by the amount of oxygen available to it. All the oxygen the body tissues receive is taken from the air by the lungs, transferred to the bloodstream and pumped round the body by the heart. The amount of oxygen that can be transferred from the air breathed into the lungs to the blood is affected by two factors. First, diseases creating abnormalities in the lungs or blood will affect the transfer of oxygen into the circulation. Second, if the air breathed in is of poor quality, for example when smoking, this reduces the concentration of oxygen breathed into the lungs. However, if a person has no underlying disease and is breathing normal fresh air, the amount of oxygen available to the body is determined by the pumping action of the heart.

The heart can increase the blood supply to the body by pumping more quickly, that is increasing the heart rate. Or it can increase the 'stroke volume', that is, the amount of blood pumped at each beat. In order to do this, the heart itself needs more oxygen. The supply of oxygen to the heart is determined by the blood flow in the coronary arteries and the concentration of oxygen in the blood. At rest the heart extracts about 65 per cent of the available oxygen in the blood, so much of the higher oxygen demand during exercise must be met by increased blood flow. If the coronary artery blood supply is unable to meet the oxygen demands of the heart muscle angina occurs, since angina is caused by too little oxygen reaching the heart muscle.

Therefore, the fitness of a person with angina is limited by the blood supply to the heart muscle. This does not mean that people with angina cannot exercise or work. It does mean that there is a point at which the heart cannot increase its output, and to continue to demand that it does brings about the symptoms of angina. So, you can work and exercise just like anyone else, as long as you do so within your comfortable limit. In addition, by taking moderate regular exercise it is possible to improve fitness and extend that limit.

How can exercise help your angina and your health?

Your heart

Becoming fit produces changes in the heart and blood circulation system. These changes include lowered heart rate at rest, lowered heart rate and blood pressure during exercise, and faster return to normal ranges of heart rate and blood pressure after exercise. These changes are collectively referred to as 'the training effect'. The result of the training effect is that for a given level of exercise the heart beats more slowly but with a larger stroke volume and therefore maintains the flow of blood from the heart known as *cardiac output*. This benefits the heart because the work of the heart is reduced. If the work of the heart is reduced by the training effect the heart muscle requires less oxygen (for a given level of exercise) and yet coronary artery blood flow is increased. This is because the coronary blood flow occurs between heartbeats so if the heart beats more slowly there is more time for blood to flow. The result is that a person with angina has an increased capacity for exercise, that is, fewer symptoms for the same amount of exercise.

Your muscles, bones and joints

Regular exercise produces many other changes which are also to the advantage of the angina sufferer. Oxygen delivery to the working muscle is improved by an increase in the number of small vessels feeding blood to the muscle. These blood vessels, called capillaries, are the very small blood vessels within the tissues where oxygen transfer takes place. Also the ability of the muscle to use oxygen is improved. The muscle cells are able to take more oxygen out of each drop of blood and so increase the oxygen uptake from the same amount of blood. The improved blood supply and more efficient use of oxygen in the skeletal muscle leads to improved strength and endurance, or *stamina*. This means the muscles become less tired during exercise and this increases the range of activities that can be enjoyed without strain.

Exercise is essential for the health of bones, ligaments, muscles and tendons. All these parts of the body need sufficient stress and strain placed on them during the regular movement and exercise of everyday life to keep them healthy.

Our bodies are very adaptable. For example, if we regularly do heavy manual work our body tissues respond. The muscles become larger and stronger, the joints become more supple and the bones become denser and stronger at the points of stress. This enables the body to cope with the extra demands being made. However, the body adapts in reverse if minimal demands are made. It is easy to appreciate the consequence of inactivity on the body if you imagine a limb that has been in plaster. The limb looks thin and feels weak because the muscles have wasted. The joints feel stiff and may be uncomfortable to move because ligaments have shortened and sometimes the bone itself becomes thinner because calcium in the bone is absorbed by the body in the absence of stress. This is known as *osteoporosis*. Of course these changes may be made worse by the injury that necessitated the plaster, but they will occur even in a perfectly healthy limb or an athlete's limb if it is deprived of normal movement.

These changes occur in the inactive person and many of the changes in the muscles and bones that we associate with old age are in fact a result of disuse. Generally as we get older we demand less of our bodies so that muscle weakness, joint stiffness and decreased exercise capacity are expected as we age. It is true that a gradual loss of muscle strength due to diminished nerve supply does occur with age. It is also true that a much larger proportion of the loss of capacity, strength and endurance is due to profound underuse and these effects are largely reversible with exercise. So exercise can be thought of as an apparent rejuvenator or at least as a way of staving off the ageing process!

Your body weight

Another important benefit of regular exercise is that it helps to prevent excessive weight gain. An overweight person puts much more stress on their heart as well as their bones and joints. An overweight person is also more 'at risk' for high blood pressure (hypertension) and diabetes. A person becomes overweight because the amount of food eaten exceeds the amount burned up by the body as fuel and the surplus is stored as fat under the skin. With all the refined and processed food (containing high energy sugar and fat) available today, coupled with the modern sedentary lifestyle, it is all too easy to put on weight (see chapter 10). Exercise can help in many ways. First, exercise uses up energy which will help to redress the balance between the amount of calories in the food eaten and the amount of calories used up by the body, so helping you to keep a steady body weight. If you are already overweight and want to reduce, then changes to your diet are needed (see Chapter 10) and these can be aided by exercise. If you take less food in but increase energy requirements by exercise, the body will use some of its fat stores to make up the balance. In addition, if you are busy with activities there is less time in which to be tempted to nibble between meals. However, if you are *very* overweight, exercise must be undertaken very cautiously, because of the extra strain your weight puts on your heart, and you should discuss it first with your doctor.

Your blood cholesterol

Exercise can also help to reduce the level of fats or cholesterol in your blood. As we saw in Chapter 1, there are two types of cholesterol known as High Density Lipoprotein (HDL) and Low Density Lipoprotein (LDL). The ratio of these two types is important – a higher ratio of HDL in the blood is thought to reduce the risk of heart disease, whereas a higher level of LDL is thought to increase the risk. Poor diet in the form of high fat intake, being overweight and lack of exercise can contribute to an increased level of LDL. However, the good news is that some studies[1,2,3] on physically active people have shown an overall lowering of blood cholesterol and a higher ratio of HDL in the blood. So exercise together with a sensible diet can help to keep the level of harmful fats in the blood under control.

Your sense of well-being

Although studies on the psychological benefits of exercise have produced mixed evidence,[4] many people who take regular exercise feel there are personal benefits of exercise above and beyond how much it benefits the body. For example, many feel that it is a way of combating stress. It helps them to unwind after a busy day at work and to forget about the stresses and strains of the day. It is uncertain whether exercise alone can produce these benefits or whether other factors that occur with exercise such as the change of surroundings, socializing and diversion are just as influential. It is true, however, that once you have found an activity that you enjoy, exercising can become a stimulating hobby and a pleasure in itself.

Points to remember about exercise

There are three main points to remember about exercise and several minor ones. The main points are that it should be safe, it should be fun and it should be regular.

Exercise should be safe

You should learn how much you can do before symptoms arise and how to identify warning signals, e.g. tightness, shortness of breath, etc. So the way to keep exercise safe is to listen to your body. To ignore symptoms is highly dangerous and *never* try to 'work off' or 'work through' pain or discomfort.

The warning signals for a person with angina are pain, pressure or tightness in the chest, uncomfortable breathing or difficulty catching your breath, or any unusual sensations. These are a signal to stop exercising immediately. Of course, during exercise you expect to breathe a little more rapidly, your heart to pump more quickly and your muscles to ache to some extent, but it should never be excessive. Be guided by your knowledge of how your body usually responds to exercise and if in doubt about the messages your body is sending, you should stop exercising and discuss the matter with your doctor.

It is much better to plan your activity from the beginning so you can avoid getting into a situation where you have to carry on when you are already tired in order to get home. It is also helpful to plan to exercise to just below when you think you would get symptoms rather than to exercise until symptoms appear. If your body says that it has had enough, stop. Fitness can be achieved just as well by moderate effort as it can be by near-maximum effort – it will just take a little longer.

Pulse taking is often recommended as a method of monitoring exercise levels but if you want to take your pulse, which is a measure of your heart rate, use it as a guide to stop you from exercising anywhere near the rate at which you get symptoms. DO NOT use it to increase your activity to achieve a pre-determined level. Sometimes the term *age predicted maximum heart rate* is used in conjunction with levels of exercise and pulse taking. The age predicted maximum heart rate is an estimate of the maximum number of heart beats your heart could manage in one minute for your age. The capacity of the heart to beat very quickly declines with age. You can work out your age predicted maximum heart rate using the following formula:

220 minus your age.

For example, if you are 53 years old:

220 − 53 = 167 beats per minute.

It is important to understand that this formula is an estimate of

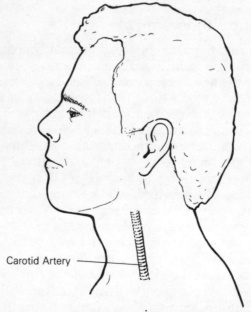

Fig 27: Position of carotid artery

your maximum heart rate for your age and not an actual rate, which could be 20 beats above or below it. For this reason do not use it to set a target for exercise; rather, use it as a guide.

As a rough guide, even if you feel very good, do not exercise above ¾ of your age predicted maximum. If you are taking beta-blockers or other heart drugs which artificially reduce heart rate, you will not be able to use this formula, but you could still use the heart rate at which you get symptoms as a marker and exercise below it.

Some people are taught to take their pulse by feeling their *carotid artery* in the side of the neck (Fig 27) but pressure on this artery can cause sudden slowing of the heart and a fall in blood pressure resulting in a blackout. Most people should be able to take their pulse in the *radial artery* in the wrist (Fig 28) which is very safe. It is easy to learn to do. Place your fingertips lightly over the shallow dip on the front of the opposite wrist just below the mound of the thumb. Count each pulse over thirty seconds and double it to get the number of beats per minute.

The best form of exercise is the type which includes free rhythmical movement provided by large muscle groups in the body. Walking, cycling and swimming are all examples of this type of exercise known as *dynamic* or *isotonic* exercise. Taking regular dynamic exercise results in the benefits to the body discussed earlier. On the other hand, exercise where the muscles contract strongly but are prevented from moving, known as *isometric* or *static* exercise, is less suitable. Examples of isometric exercise are weightlifting and push-ups. This form of exercise can produce a sudden undesirable increase in blood pressure and workload on the heart. You should also avoid any home activity where you are pushing or pulling and therefore straining

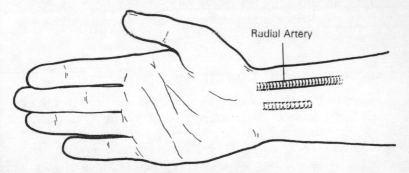

Fig 28: Position of radial artery

against a very heavy or immobile object such as pushing the car
or shovelling snow.

Exercise should be fun

Exercise is of little or no use if it is regarded as something
unpleasant or boring that you have to do. The exercise you
choose should be comfortable and within your capabilities,
interesting and most of all, enjoyable. There is such a variety of
activities available now that there is something to suit everyone,
however limited their exercise capacity may be. Many forms of
exercise, for example, rambling, bowls and golf are also social
activities providing the opportunity to meet people and make
new friends as well as providing opportunities for physical
exercise.

If possible, choose several varieties of exercise so that you do
not become bored. Weather conditions may prevent you from
pursuing certain activities sometimes, so a variety ensures that
some form of exercise is always available whatever the weather.

Exercise is more enjoyable and there is less chance of injury
if you are competent at the techniques of your chosen activity.
It is not necessary to become an expert, but it is a good idea to
do some background reading of books which are now available
on even the most exotic of sports and or to get some practical
help from more practised players.

Try to avoid competitive exercise as this adds a stressful
element to the activity. It is sometimes difficult to stop exercising
if it means letting down friends or team mates, and the pressures
of competition may encourage you to continue exercising after
you know you should stop.

Think about taking up an entirely new sport or activity that
suits your interests and level of exertion. It could add a new
dimension to your life.

Exercise should be regular

In order to gain the benefits that exercise can offer it must be
performed regularly. It is important to remember this when
choosing your activity, because those which require the hire of
special equipment or which involve travel may not be practicable on a regular basis. Aim to do 20–30 minutes of exercise
three times a week and gradually build up the intensity of the

exercise. This will be sufficient to produce the adaptions of the training effect over a period of time between 6–12 weeks.[5,6,7] Remember that fitness cannot be stored, it needs to be maintained by regular exercise. if you stop exercising for two or three weeks the training effect will gradually decline and fitness will be lost. For example, if you played sport at school, think how you ached after the first match of the term in comparison with the last match. That was because you had lost fitness before the first match during the holidays, but by the last match of the term you had played regularly and gained fitness.

There is absolutely no advantage in overexercising. It is only necessary to do just a little bit more than you would normally do to benefit. Indeed, the less fit you are when you start, the more you will improve and the more you will notice the benefits. It is a dangerous myth that exercise should hurt or 'burn'. The stiffness is caused by the buildup of lactic acid in the muscles as described on page 132. Generally, stiffness in the muscles should be avoided but if your muscles do become stiff after a period of exercise, allow the stiffness to go before the next session. Low-intensity exercise such as gentle walking may help to disperse the stiffness.

Other hints about exercise

It is best not to exercise after a heavy meal when food is being digested
During digestion the body diverts a large amount of blood to the blood vessels in the gut. This is so that nutrients from the digested food can be absorbed into the blood for use by the body's tissues and organs. The heart rate and cardiac output are higher during digestion in order to cope with this diversion of blood to the gut and remain so up to 4 hours after eating a large meal, even at rest. So exercising directly after a large meal puts extra strain on the heart.

Avoid exercising after consuming alcohol
This too increases the heart rate.

Take note of the weather conditions
Strong winds or low temperatures can trigger an angina attack even without exercise. Very hot or humid weather will make it

difficult for you to lose enough heat, which can make you feel uncomfortable or overtired. If it is very hot or humid, exercise during the early morning or in the evening when it is cooler. If the weather is wet or cold choose an indoor activity such as gentle 'keep fit' exercises which can be done at home or go to your local sports centre or swimming baths.

Wear the correct clothing and footwear

This does not necessarily mean that you have to spend a fortune on specialist or trendy sports clothes. Indeed, comfortable loose clothing and well-fitting rubber-soled shoes which support the arch of your foot may be all that you need for your chosen activity. On the other hand, if you do require specific equipment or sportswear, get advice from people who are knowledgeable about the sport. It may save you time and money in the long run. Many sports clubs sell second-hand equipment or have loan facilities so that you can try the sport before you commit yourself to investing in all the accompanying paraphernalia.

Do not exercise if you feel unwell and especially if you have a viral infection

This includes common viral infections such as a cold or influenza. Viral infections can cause inflammation of the heart muscle or myocardium which is called *myocarditis*. Exercise will greatly increase the problem and could cause permanent damage to the heart.

Remember the maxim 'moderation in all things'

All forms of extreme behaviour are detrimental. There is no virtue in overexercising or in becoming obsessed with your health.

Coping with everyday activities

Driving

After a heart attack a person is not permitted to hold an HGV licence. There is usually no reason why a person with angina should not continue to drive a car. However, it is prudent to plan ahead, if possible, to avoid unnecessary stress which might provoke an attack.

Try to avoid rush-hour traffic, especially if you are driving anywhere for the first time and do not know your way. It only adds stress to an already difficult situation. Leave plenty of time for a journey if you are driving to a specific appointment. If you do get stuck in a jam or there is some other hold-up, worrying about being late only compounds the problem. Instead of becoming angry, frustrated or worried in traffic jams, use the time to do some simple relaxation as outlined in Chapter 7.

If you have to drive a very long way, arrange to stay somewhere overnight to halve the journey. Or try to break up the travelling with regular stops to stretch your legs and keep you fresh. Try not to drive when you are tired, as this increases stress.

If you are driving to an unfamiliar place, make a plan of your route before you go so that you know which roads and turnings to take. Better still, take someone with you to navigate. It is all too common to experience the panic of approaching a sign on a busy motorway or trunk road and not recognizing any of the road numbers!

If you do get chest pain or discomfort whilst you are driving, pull over to the side as soon as you can safely do so. Stop the car and rest. Concentrate on using a relaxation technique until the discomfort goes. Let someone else continue the driving if possible but if by yourself don't continue your journey until you feel perfectly comfortable.

Sex

Sexual intercourse, like any other form of exercise, can provoke an angina attack, especially since it involves muscular activity combined with a high level of excitement and emotion. However, it is usually estimated that if a person can climb two flights of stairs or take a brisk walk round the block without symptoms, they can cope with the amount of exertion needed for sexual intercourse.

As with any exercise, it is wise to reduce additional stress and for this reason avoid sex if you are tired or emotionally upset. Avoid intercourse after a heavy meal or consumption of alcohol. Sex with different partners or extra-marital affairs puts more strain on the heart than that with familiar partners.

Some medications such as beta-blockers prescribed by your doctor for angina may reduce the sex drive and if this is a problem discuss it with your doctor who may be able to suggest alternative drugs (see Chapter 2). If intercourse does provoke angina, medication which helps to prevent angina attacks, such as GTN, may be helpful for use just before sex. Again this is something you should discuss with your doctor (see Chapter 2).

Work

The amount of exercise a person performs in their job depends of course on the type of job. All the hints and advice about recreational exercise apply equally to exercise at work. The main difference is the stress generated by work such as deadlines, responsibility for other employees, dealing with customers and so on. If yours is a high-stress job it is important that you learn how to cope so as to minimize its effect on the heart (see Chapters 3 to 7).

Recommended exercise

The amount of exercise that can be performed safely and comfortably will be different for each person. Factors such as the speed of onset and severity of your symptoms, the type of medication you take, whether you have problems with your back or joints, your age, sex and body weight will all influence the amount of activity you can cope with. However, one exercise which is ideal in nearly every way and which practically everyone can manage is walking.

Walking

Walking is a safe and natural exercise.

Perhaps the only problem with walking is that it is such a natural activity that people may not regard it as 'proper' exercise! It does not require special skills or equipment, except for a good pair of shoes, and you can do it anywhere. The great thing about walking is that it *is* so adaptable. The speed you go and the distance you cover is entirely up to you and can be modified whenever you want so it can always be kept safe and comfortable.

As with any exercise, start gently and gradually build up. Start by increasing the distance you walk. Later, when you have found the distance that is suitable for you, increase the pace. You will eventually find a pace at which you feel comfortable but at which you are working quite hard. You should never push the pace until you feel exhausted, short of breath or feel pain in the chest. You should prepare for exercise by using rapid relaxation (see Chapter 7).

Once you know what you can cope with, try fitting your walking into your everyday life. For example, if you normally take a bus to and from the shops try walking there and catching the bus home, or if practicable try walking all or part of the way to work. Walking is often the key to other pursuits such as rambling or golf.

You may find it helpful to make a record of your walking so that you can see how you are progressing. Pedometers are small gauges which clip onto your waist and measure the distance you have walked. They are not too expensive and are available from most sports shops.

In conclusion, walking is a cheap, safe, enjoyable and readily available form of exercise. It uses the large muscle groups in the body in rhythmical movement and provided it is done regularly with gradual increase in distance and pace it is an efficient way of improving fitness.

Stairs

Climbing stairs is another very effective way of exercising for although it requires more effort than walking it can be adapted to suit individual needs. The speed at which you climb stairs and the number you climb should be designed to give you exercise without causing symptoms. Start slowly and gradually increase the number of steps. The easiest way to do this at home is to step up and down on the bottom step of the stairs and either keep count of the number you do or time the duration of the exercise. This means you can keep track of your progress. In addition stair climbing is useful if adverse weather conditions keep you indoors and prevents your usual exercise. It is also a good idea to fit it into everyday life. For example, if you have a choice when you are at work or out shopping use the stairs instead of taking a lift or if it is further than you can manage, walk up part of the way and use the lift for the remainder. Remember always keep your exercise at a comfortable level.

Other common forms of exercise include jogging, cycling, swimming and keep fit.

Jogging

There is no more to be gained by jogging that cannot be achieved by brisk walking in terms of fitness. Walking will just take a little longer. But if you do want to jog it is essential to wear a good pair of trainers which have thick shock-absorbing soles since jogging causes much more jarring in the hip, knee and ankle joints than walking.

Many people with angina may find that although they can walk for a good distance, jogging soon brings them to their exercise limit. Remember that it is better to exercise for longer at say, only half your limit than to do only a minute or two at near maximum before you have to stop. This is because exercising for such a short period would not be enough to increase fitness, and in any case it is harmful to push yourself to the maximum. So, for many people with angina jogging will not be suitable.

Cycling

Cycling is very good exercise. It uses large groups of muscles in a smooth rhythmical movement and does not jar the joints in the legs. If only the world was flat it would be perfect! Unfortunately, for the person with angina, apart from the obvious hazards of coping with traffic, slopes and hills can present a problem. Just as a car engine has to work harder and uses more fuel when going uphill, so does the body. This means the heart has to work harder to get oxygen to the working leg muscles and in doing so needs more oxygen itself. As previously described in this chapter, if the oxygen demand of the heart is greater than the oxygen supply to the heart, the symptoms of angina are felt.

However, one way round the traffic and the gradient problem is to use a stationary exercise bike. You can use it in or out of doors so the weather is no problem and you can set as much or as little resistance as you want to pedal against. To start with, set the resistance very low so it feels as if you are cycling along the flat. Pedal smoothly at the rate of about one revolution per second and gradually build up the time until you can pedal for fifteen to twenty minutes. If you can do that comfortably you can start to increase the resistance that you are pedalling against until it feels as if you are pedalling up a gentle slope. It might take you several weeks to reach this point.

The main drawback with using exercise bicycles is that pedalling in one place for 20 minutes or so can be boring! In addition some knee conditions, especially problems with the kneecap, can become irritated by the repeated bending and straightening needed for cycling. But apart from this, cycling is a very efficient way of increasing fitness.

Swimming

Swimming is another very good form of exercise which uses large muscle groups in a rhythmical way. Swimming is often possible when joint problems make other forms of exercise difficult because the body weight is supported by the water. Other advantages of swimming are that it is not affected by the weather, and you can choose how hard and for how long you want to swim.

On the other hand it is not as convenient as exercise that can be done at home and of course you need to be able to swim! As with all the other exercises that have been mentioned, start very gently and build up gradually. This is very important, as it would be more dangerous to provoke an angina attack in the water where you may be out of your depth, than, for example, out walking where you could immediately stop or sit down. It is a good idea to take somebody with you the first few times, both for company and to assist you if you do have any symptoms. However, you will soon discover what you can comfortably do.

Keep fit

There are many forms of 'keep fit' ranging from aerobics, which tends to be fast and furious and therefore not suitable for most people with angina, to much gentler bending and strengthening exercises. If you find a class which suits you, tell the instructor that you have angina and that you will go at your own pace and stop if necessary. Don't be pressurized by being in a group to do more than your body will comfortably let you. Avoid exercises which make you strain or hold your breath because it means they are too strong for you. For example, sit-ups are very strenuous, especially for women, and if you are straining to do them, apart from the danger of hurting the stomach muscles you may be straining the heart by severely increasing the blood pressure. Another unsuitable exercise involves lying on your back and lifting both legs in a straight position off the floor. This is too hard for most people and may cause strain to the stomach, the back and the heart.

If your joints are a bit stiff then gentle swinging or rhythmic movements are generally good. They help to lubricate the joints and make them more mobile. However, if you have a back problem, repeated bending and touching the toes is harmful and will make the condition worse. If in doubt about the exercise you are doing, get advice from your doctor or physiotherapist.

Of course there are hundreds of different activities besides the few described. Use your common sense and be guided by what has already been said in terms of safety, frequency and duration.

Avoid highly competitive sport which may incite you to do more than is comfortable. If you are changing altitudes rapidly, allow time to acclimatize. If your angina is stress-induced then activities such as hang-gliding and ski jumping are not for you! Avoid the type of exercise which pushes you up to your limit very quickly. Remember you are aiming to do about twenty minutes of exercise comfortably. But, most important of all, enjoy your exercise and have fun doing it.

CHAPTER 9

Angina and smoking

If heart patients are only told to do one thing after being diagnosed, it is to 'give up smoking if you want to live'. This can seem harsh advice to heap on the unwelcome news of heart disease. It can seem like a further cost, even a penance. Moreover, giving up smoking is not as simple as such advice, so easily given, would have us believe. Giving up smoking usually requires more than simply giving up on a whim. It takes a certain amount of commitment and skill. This section of the book intends to provide you with both of these essential attributes. But first, why stop smoking . . .?

Why stop smoking?

Smoking has been shown to be a major contributory factor to many diseases.[1] Smoking as a risk factor for heart disease has been discussed elsewhere in this book. However, it can also result in a number of diseases of the lung and throat, particularly cancer, bronchitis and emphysema. It has also been associated with other types of cancer including bladder cancer, and cancer of the cervix in women.

Perhaps even more importantly, smoking can have a direct effect on the symptoms of angina. Sudden intake of nicotine can send the arteries providing oxygen to the heart into spasm, restricting the flow of oxygen to the heart muscle, and causing an attack of angina.

Carbon monoxide, also taken in cigarette smoke, reduces the amount of oxygen that can be taken up by the bloodstream, and muscles of the body, placing strain on the heart in getting enough oxygen to the body. This makes someone who smokes more likely to have angina while exercising.

So, while smoking may contribute in the long term to the development of disease, it also has a direct effect on the daily experience of the symptoms of angina. Smoking also increases the likelihood of the development of chest infections, causing breathlessness, which can increase the symptoms associated with angina.

More encouragingly, this means that stopping smoking can have immediate, and not just long-term, effects on health. Within a day of stopping, carbon monoxide leaves the body and as nicotine is no longer inhaled it can no longer contribute to any angina symptoms. As well as these immediate benefits, longer-term health benefits are that any disease process related to smoking immediately stops, and the body begins the process of repair. Stopping smoking has been shown to significantly lessen the risk of further heart attacks, with the risk of having a second heart attack reducing to the same as that of a non-smoker after 5 years.[2] Think you are past the point of no return? If you cut yourself do you stop bleeding? Of course. The body *never* loses

---

MY REASONS FOR STOPPING SMOKING NOW

Money!

Fed up of coughing up 'muck'
every morning

Avoid nagging from friends and family
(and reduce their worries about my health)

I want to enjoy my food again

My clothes will stop smelling
(and won't have any more burn holes)

No more washing out smelly ashtrays

Fig 29

its ability to repair itself and even if you have smoked for many years you can reduce the risk of further heart problems.

Of course, improvements in health are not the only benefits from stopping smoking. Smoking results in a reduced sense of smell and taste, stained teeth and fingers, bad breath and costs a fortune! If you smoke twenty cigarettes a day, you are spending hundreds of pounds a year. Stopping smoking can change all this. A hidden benefit many people find is that when they have successfully stopped smoking, they feel more confident in themselves, and their self-esteem is increased.

Many people give up smoking as a result of illness: bronchitis, angina and so on. Other give up for less obvious reasons such as having just decorated a room and not wishing to stain the wallpaper and curtains with cigarette smoke, the birth of a grandchild, changing jobs and using this as an opportunity to break old habits. Some reasons are very simple: lack of money or a birthday promise. Fig 29 provides an example from one person who gave up smoking in one of our 'stop smoking groups'.

However, these are other people's reasons for giving up smoking, and may not apply to you. Thinking about your personal reasons for wanting to stop, and writing them down can help both as a means of motivating yourself to stop, and to remind yourself of these reasons if the going gets difficult in the future. This can be an important beginning to any attempt to stop smoking, and is worth spending a few minutes thinking about.

Giving up

There are a multitude of ways to give up smoking. These vary from the use of herbal cigarette replacements, associating smoking with various unpleasant sensations such as dense cigarette smoke or even electric shocks, through to the use of acupuncture and hypnotism. Most of these require help – sometimes expensive help – from experts either directly or through the purchase of various aids to quitting.

Smoking cessation groups may be run by a variety of people including psychologists, counsellors, health education officers, and so on. They often use similar methods to those suggested in this chapter, but give the additional benefit of group support.

Sometimes, if people do not want to become part of a group the service may also take individual referrals. They are also run by a number of private clinics.

If you wish to go to a professional for help it is worth asking your own doctor to recommend an expert or smoking clinic (both private or NHS) and to refer you if possible. But be warned and take advice – not all those who practise such treatments privately (particularly hypnosis) are as skilled as perhaps one would expect, nor are their results generally better than the approaches suggested in this chapter.[3] Acupuncture is often cited as a useful aid to giving up smoking – some useful addresses are given at the end of the book. For example, the British Acupuncture Association will send you a booklet explaining acupuncture and also giving a list of registered acupuncturists.

One increasingly popular method of giving up smoking is through the use of nicotine substitutes. If you smoke regularly your body becomes used to a regular supply of nicotine. Take this away, and you can experience a number of uncomfortable symptoms as the body adjusts to having no nicotine. These are known as withdrawal symptoms – you are withdrawing from an addiction to nicotine. By taking nicotine in the form of chewing gum, without inhaling all the other poisons in cigarette smoke, some people can gradually give up smoking whilst keeping these symptoms to a minimum. Unfortunately for people with angina, the amount of nicotine in these nicotine substitutes can be enough to excite the heart, or to send the heart's arteries into spasm, just (or even more dramatically) as smoking a cigarette. This means that doctors do not recommend the use of these substitutes to heart patients.

Thankfully, there are other, equally successful, ways of giving up. The rest of this chapter takes you through some of these methods in a step-by-step guide to giving up smoking that does not require expert help or guidance.

Cutting down?

Most smokers would like gradually to cut down on their smoking each day, until eventually they find that they have cut out cigarettes completely, perhaps without even realizing it. Unfortunately few people succeed in this apparently simple and pain-free approach. Many reach a level of about ten or twelve cigarettes a day, then begin to find it hard to cut down further, and gradually creep up to their previous consumption. For this reason, most experts recommend a gradual reduction to smoking about 10 to 12 cigarettes a day, followed by stopping completely.

This is the approach that will be taken here. The time spent cutting down should be two or even three weeks, and this will provide time in which to develop strategies and skills for giving up the more difficult cigarettes.

Step 1: keeping a smoker's diary

People smoke for different reasons at different times. Sometimes it is because the body is low on nicotine, and requires an extra shot to keep us going (because of an addiction to nicotine). Sometimes it is out of habit. Many people automatically begin to light a cigarette when they answer the telephone, finish a meal, or have a drink of coffee. Often these cigarettes are not the result of the body requiring a shot of nicotine. They are smoked because something happens to trigger off what has become an automatic habit in that situation. Triggers to smoking often include:

● having a cup of coffee in the kitchen
● seeing someone else smoke
● relaxing after finishing a job of work
● being offered a cigarette by a friend
● boredom
● seeing a cigarette advertisement.

Learning to identify triggers to smoking is an important first stage to giving up. This can best be done by keeping a smoker's diary. Table 4 shows you an example of one. In this diary you can record every time you smoke, and your reasons for smoking that particular cigarette, and what triggered your smoking off. This may be a biological 'need' (or craving) for a cigarette, it may result from habit, it may be a means of trying to deal with stress, and so on.

As a means of planning to cut down, it is also possible to record how easy you think it would be to cut that cigarette out in the future. A ten-point scale is suggested, where 10 = no problem, and 0 = extremely difficult. It is best to carry the diary with you and to record each cigarette before you actually smoke it. This may be more hassle, but this can actually work for you by making you think twice before having a cigarette. Table 4 is an example from one person who gave up smoking in one of our 'stop smoking groups'.

Day	Time	Why did I smoke?	Ease of giving up
Monday	7.30	First of the day – lovely!	3
	7.45	With breakfast – habit	6
	8.37	Driving to work – boredom in traffic – even had time to fill in my diary.	7
	10.30	Coffee break – sat with smokers	5
	12.30	Lunch break – really need this one	4
	12.40	Enjoying a second one – habit really	8

Table 4

Step 2: Cutting down

After filling in a diary for a few days it should fairly quickly become clear which of the cigarettes you smoke will be relatively easy to give up, and which will be the more difficult. The next stage is to begin to cut down cigarettes, starting with some of the easier cigarettes first.

To plan how many cigarettes to cut down initially, it is necessary to decide how long you are going to take cutting down before you stop smoking altogether. This takes some serious thought as overoptimism in your planning may mean you become depressed by a failure to achieve too high a target, while too long a period may mean that you feel you are not getting anywhere. A period of between two and three weeks may be a reasonable compromise, although if you are already smoking close to ten or twelve a day (or are smoking less) a shorter period may be more appropriate. It is best to choose a time (if possible) when you can expect not to be under any special stress or strain. People often resort to tried-and-tested methods of coping with stress (usually including smoking) at such times. Of course, you cannot always predict future stresses. One person attending our 'stop smoking' groups felt so stressed whilst workmen ran into a series of disasters building an extension to her house that she never gave up. But do try!

After you have decided on the period of cutting down, cut down in three similar-sized reductions over the period you have chosen, so that you are down to ten to twelve a day before you are ready to stop completely.

During this period of cutting down it is important to continue with the smoker's diary that you may have started in Step 1. It can be used to identify which triggers to your smoking are still problems. It can also help you to plan how you will cope with those triggers when you stop smoking completely. It may also be useful in helping you cope when you do not smoke a cigarette at a time that you previously would have done.

There are a number of tactics you can use to cope with triggers to smoking. One simple tactic is to avoid or alter situations that trigger your smoking, and make them different so they do not trigger smoking, or do not allow you to smoke. Here are some examples:

Avoiding triggers

At work:

- sit in a different part of the canteen or recreation room with non-smokers
- do not carry cigarettes around with you so you cannot smoke
- go for a walk during breaks

At home:

- If you keep cigarettes in the house, keep them somewhere inaccessible so it takes some effort to get them
- hide all the ashtrays
- ask your partner not to mention smoking (however well you are doing)

On the move:

- if you go by bus, travel in the no smoking area
- if you travel by car, keep your cigarettes in the boot, or empty out the ashtrays

Socially:

- visit friends who do not smoke
- sit in the no smoking area of the cinema or theatre
- avoid 'borrowing' cigarettes to kid yourself you don't smoke because you don't carry a packet around with you

Coping with triggers

Unless you become a hermit, it is almost impossible to avoid all triggers to smoking. It is therefore worth planning some ways to deal with triggers to smoking. Below are a number of suggestions:

- Practise saying 'No thank you – I don't smoke' in the mirror in the morning, before you go out with friends who smoke. Practice makes perfect!
- Particularly when you are cutting down, don't get involved in 'rounds' of cigarettes. This will only lead to pressure to smoke more.
- Try to do something else instead of smoking – try chewing sugar-free gum, eating fresh fruit and so on.
- Concentrate hard on other things going on around you to distract from temptation to smoke.

These are suggestions that many people have made and found useful. Again, they may not be appropriate or the best for you. As you go through the phase of cutting down, each time you have a cigarette try to think how you would have coped with that temptation if you were not smoking, or if you chose to cut that one out as part of the cutting down. As you develop these plans, you can bring them into use as you cut down.

Step 3: Stopping completely

After cutting down to about ten cigarettes a day, the next phase is to give up completely. It is at this stage that any withdrawal effects are likely to be encountered. These may be unpleasant, and a few ideas about how to cope with them are given below. However, it is worth looking at exactly what these effects are before looking at means of coping with them. They are a sign of the body beginning to recover from nicotine poisoning. Poison? Yes, nicotine is a very powerful poison – one drop of pure nicotine placed on your tongue would kill you. Although unpleasant, withdrawal symptoms are actually a sign of the beginning of the body's recovery. Indeed, another way of looking at withdrawal symptoms is to think of them as 'symptoms of recovery'.

Not everyone suffers from these symptoms, which include shakiness, sweating, restlessness, poor sleep and concentration. If they do have them, they normally last two or three weeks, although the first two or three days are usually the worst – after this, things get easier. The most common withdrawal symptom is the craving for a cigarette. However, even at their worst these cravings are not continuous. They come in peaks lasting two or three minutes, with periods of calm in between.

As time goes on the time between the peaks and their intensity decreases, until they stop being a problem. It is these peaks which you need to learn to cope with. Below are some suggestions that some people who succeeded in giving up smoking found useful:

- Try to accept any discomfort in a positive way. Each period of discomfort represents your body getting back to normality.
- If you can, go and clean your teeth and gargle. This may help to distract you from the discomfort, and make your mouth fresh so you don't want a cigarette.
- Try to relax as much as you can, and concentrate your mind on a pleasant, soothing image.
- Remind yourself that the feelings will not last forever, and will become easier to cope with.
- Eat fruit, sugar-free gum, drink water or fruit juice – anything to occupy your taste buds until the craving goes.
- Do not carry cigarettes on you, so that however great the temptation, you cannot succumb.

Again, these are approaches that have helped other people cope with withdrawal symptoms. It may be worth thinking of a few more – perhaps thinking back to any previous attempt to stop smoking may help you come up with some suitable ideas.

Giving up for life

This can be the most difficult stage, certainly in the first few days. For this reason, it is often encouraging to reward yourself for any success you achieve. This may vary from a glow of self-satisfaction at the end of a smoke-free day to real rewards for varying degrees of success. For example, a trip to the cinema

---

CONTRACT

I declare that I

_____John Stephens_____

intend to give up smoking on

_____1st June 1989_____

and that

_____Mary Goldsmith_____

promises to give me support and encouragement
in support of my new smoke-free existence and
better health

Signature of smoker

Signature of supporter

Date

---

after one successful day (sitting in the no smoking zone, of course!), a meal in a restaurant after giving up for a week, and so on.

Some people feel it is rather self-indulgent to reward themselves for making such progress. But giving up smoking is a real and difficult achievement and needs to be adequately rewarded. It may be useful to think of a few rewards to give yourself over the next few days, or even weeks. You may as well get some pleasure out of giving up!

The planning stage is now complete, and now is the time for putting it all into practice. The skills of coping with triggers, plans to avoid them if practicable, and methods of dealing with any withdrawal symptoms can now be put into full action. During the next few days make one day the day you stop smoking, your QUIT DAY.

To mark this day, and to help you maintain your will-power over the next few days or weeks, make a contract with yourself to stop on your quit day. To help gain support during this time it can be useful to enrol a relative or friend into a contract to give you support as well. This will gain you support, but also make your commitment public and give you a bit of extra incentive to stop. A typical contract is shown here.

During the first few days after your quit day, try to avoid as many triggers to smoking as possible, gradually going back to them as you gain in confidence. When you cannot avoid triggers, use all the coping strategies you have rehearsed during the past few days or weeks. Remember, the first two or three days are generally the worst – after this it does get easier.

During the next few days it is worth carrying your diary along with you, so that if nothing else, the empty pages can be a source of pride, and if you do have a cigarette you can write why you had that cigarette, and use this to plan how to cope in that situation should it arise again. A few extra ideas for coping over the next few days:

- When the time comes to stop smoking, keep the last cigarette in your mouth all the time, so that the smoke and smell gets in your eyes. Make your last experience with cigarettes an unpleasant one.
- Don't forget to involve family and friends – their help may be crucial.
- If your will-power wanes during the week, have a look at your

YOUR CONTRACT

I declare that I

_____

intend to give up smoking on

_____

and that

_____

promises to give me support and encouragement
in support of my new smoke-free existence and
better health

Signature of smoker

Signature of supporter

Date

---

reasons for wanting to stop now. Write two main reasons on
a card and look at the card every time you have a drink of tea
or coffee.
- Try to keep busy, not just with work but with things you enjoy,
for a few days so that you have less time to think about
cigarettes.

Planning for weak moments
It is worth remembering an emergency drill should you succumb

to a cigarette. If you should smoke a cigarette after you have made the decision to stop, take a few minutes to think upon the following lines:

- 'To err is human.' To have one cigarette does not mean that all your hard work has been in vain, or that you have no will-power. It also does not mean that you have to continue smoking.
- Be honest and admit that you have made a mistake. But use this to your advantage. Make a commitment to learn from your mistake so that you can avoid it in the future.
- Try not to feel guilty, frustrated, or discouraged. If you do, tell yourself that these feelings will pass.
- Stop smoking NOW. Not tomorrow, not next week. Avoid the cop-out response of 'Since I smoked today I might as well go ahead and smoke as much as I want and stop smoking tomorrow.' There is always the danger that tomorrow never comes.

Any notes you have made in this book, or in the diary, contain tactics to help you quit. If you have any last-minute worries before quitting, it may be worth spending a few minutes trying to think of any solutions to any problems you foresee. It is better to spend time now than to try to think when you are in the thick of things.

Step 4: Staying stopped

Staying stopped actually has two phases. The first is coping with the few weeks after you have got past the initial few days of giving up. This entails using the skills you have already developed, while dealing with a few extra issues. The second involves thinking more into the future about ways to avoid slipping back to smoking again.

Filling time

Many people who give up smoking feel that something is missing from their life. It leaves almost a feeling of emptiness. It can be hard to replace a habit that you have had for many years. Unfortunately, if that hole is not filled with something new, smoking may come back to fill it. For this reason, it is well worth spending some time thinking about other pleasurable ways you can spend your time in the future instead of smoking. You may think of taking a new interest, or taking up an old one again.

The following list of questions may help you to generate ideas.

● What do you enjoy learning?
● What day trips do you enjoy?
● What do you enjoy doing on your own?
● What do you enjoy doing with others?
● What do you enjoy that costs nothing?
● What do you enjoy that costs less than five pounds?

The list is as long as your imagination. If you can think of an alternative to smoking, this will give you a fighting chance of staying off 'the weed' for ever.

Staying healthy

Two other skills that can help during this early period are relaxation and sensible eating. Relaxation can help you to cope better with any stress that caused you to smoke, and with any that results from giving up, such as irritability or feeling unable to relax. Sensible eating can help prevent any weight gain that may occur as you give up. This may happen firstly because nicotine reduces the uptake of sugar from the gut, and therefore when you stop smoking more of the calories you take in are available to your body. Perhaps more important, however, is that smoking directly (and indirectly as food loses its taste) reduces appetite. Thus people who give up often simply eat more food than before. Ways of eating sensibly and losing weight are looked at in other parts of the book and will not be examined here in detail.

However, it is perhaps worth mentioning that smoking is far more damaging to the heart than being overweight. Some people do gain weight after they stop smoking. However, the benefits of stopping smoking far outweigh any problems linked to an increase in weight.

It is difficult to stop smoking and cut down eating at the same time. As a rule of thumb, it is better to lose any weight gain a few weeks after you have stopped smoking (and are feeling confident in keeping off cigarettes) than trying to do both at the same time. You should then be able to do this using the sensible eating guidelines outlined in Chapter 10.

Some final ideas

Just as planning can help you to stop smoking, it may also help you to remain a non-smoker. The skills you needed to get you through the difficult first few days or even weeks can also help you in the future if the temptation to smoke arises. Your smoker's diary may give you some indication of times that you need to be particularly careful in the future. It is worth occasionally reminding yourself of any tactics that were especially useful to you in coping with them. Below are a few more tactics that you may find helpful to staying off cigarettes permanently.

- Avoid complacency. One of the commonest reasons for starting to smoke again is that people simply 'felt like a cigarette', had 'just one or two' and became hooked on smoking again.
- Be careful of situations in which you previously smoked. In particular, be careful if you previously smoked when drinking. Alcohol is a well-known destroyer of good resolutions. Before going out for a drink, think about how you will cope with any temptation. Remember to say 'NO'.
- Tell people if they offer you a cigarette that you don't smoke, not that you've given up. It sounds more positive and discourages them from offering you cigarettes that you may find difficult to turn down.
- Remember 'the con'. Every time you see an advertisement for cigarettes, or see them for sale in the tobacconist, remember that someone has spent vast amounts of money to tempt you to ruin your health and to provide them with profits. Enjoy the fact that you are no longer taken in by the con.
- Mark a day in your diary to look back every month at the benefits you have gained by not smoking. Better health, pride, as well as financial rewards are within your grasp.
- Be prepared to cope with craving. Some ex-smokers report that they have occasional strong urges to smoke. These do not last very long, and no one is really sure why they occur, but be prepared.
- Remember, if you do have a cigarette, avoid the cop-out response. We all make mistakes. Stop smoking NOW. Not tomorrow, not next week – because tomorrow never comes.

And finally . . . enjoy life as a non-smoker.

CHAPTER 10

Angina and your diet

In this chapter we are going to look at the importance of your diet for your heart. What you eat, why you eat what you eat and why you may be reluctant to change.

Secondly, this chapter will explain what you should eat and ways of making changes to enable you to adapt to a healthier lifestyle which will make you leaner, fitter and more able to face the rigours of life.

What is wrong with our diet? Is what we eat important?

Many scientific studies have demonstrated the link between what we eat and the diseases we may suffer from, for example, Coronary Heart Disease (CHD) which is linked to eating too much fat, in particular, saturated fat (animal fat). A study was made by Ansel Keys[1] in which he looked at men in Japan, Greece, Yugoslavia, Italy, the Netherlands, USA and Finland. The findings were that countries which have high levels of CHD such as the USA and Finland consume relatively large amounts of saturated fat and have high levels of cholesterol in their blood. Countries such as Japan and Greece which have relatively low levels of CHD consume much lower amounts of saturated fat and have lower levels of cholesterol in their blood. This research began to link CHD with diet and the amount of cholesterol in our blood.

A large research study in Framingham, Massachusetts, USA looked at what happens if you follow a group of middle-aged men for a period of several years and monitor their level of cholesterol and the rate of CHD. They found that the higher the level of cholesterol, the higher the rate of CHD, again demonstrating the link between cholesterol and heart disease. [2]

The question then asked was what happens if you lower a person's blood cholesterol? Does this reduce their chance of developing CHD? It has been demonstrated in many studies, using both drugs and diet to reduce blood cholesterol, that in fact it does.

In the Los Angeles Veterans Administrative Study, [3] 846 male volunteers aged 55–89 received either a typical North American diet or a reduced fat diet, similar to the one explained in this chapter. The men were then followed for 8 years. It was found that cholesterol was reduced by 13 per cent, and deaths due to the furring up of arteries were very much reduced, in those who had been receiving the reduced fat diet.

How does all this help you if you are suffering from angina?

Further studies now show that reducing your level of cholesterol may halt the furring up of your blood vessels. For example, research in Helsinki, Finland [4] looked at 36 men and 2 women with coronary artery disease, while on a special diet. They succeeded in reducing their cholesterol, and they were then monitored for a period of seven years. The results were then compared with a group of men and women, also with coronary artery disease, but who had not reduced their cholesterol level. The results demonstrated that the furring up of the arteries in those with reduced cholesterol levels progressed more slowly than those who had not reduced their cholesterol. So reducing your cholesterol by controlling your diet may prevent your heart disease from getting worse.

Do we know what we should eat?

Most of us know the Healthy Eating messages. We know that eating too much fat is bad for our hearts. We know that sugar and sweets will rot our teeth and may make us fat. We know that eating too much food and taking too little exercise is the reason we get overweight, *so why do we do it*? We know that we should eat more fibre, more bread, vegetables and fruit. We know that if we could only eat 'Healthy Food' we would be leaner, fitter and healthier, *so why don't we do it*?

Why do people with angina find it hard to eat healthily?

There are many reasons:

- We may not know how to cook healthily.
- We may be worried that the shopping bills will rise.
- We may be worried that the family will complain about 'strange food'.
- The local shops may only have a limited selection of food.
- We may be trying to eat less fat but are not sure which foods are low in fat.
- We may be baffled by the food labels.
- We may be unsure of what *is* healthy when so many things seem to be bad for us.
- We may be just stuck in our ways!
- We may feel that one of the big problems is that the experts are always changing their minds.
- We seem to read a different story in the paper every week.

Write down/make a list of any problems you have experienced in trying to change to a healthier diet.

The next section explores the roots of some of your eating habits.

Changing advice

There has been a major change in advice about which foods are considered healthy in the last 10–20 years. Think about these foods.

- Milk
- Cheese
- Butter
- Bread
- Potatoes
- Meat
- Eggs

Have your ideas about whether these foods are 'good for you' or 'bad for you' changed at all over the years?

How have your ideas changed?

A summary of current expert advice on the relevance of what we eat to people with angina is discussed on page 171-2. But it is common to find people vary in what they believe the experts say – so it is not surprising that people find it difficult to know how to eat healthily.

Family traditions and food habits

Our food habits are formed when we are children, and like all habits they can be very hard to change.

Try to remember back to when you were 10 years old, and picture a school day in the middle of winter. Jot down any memories of food that come into your mind.

- What would you have had for breakfast?
- Did you have lunch at school? Jot down some memories of school meals.

Jot down foods you liked best – look at the list – which words would you use to describe them? Are they mostly sweet, stodgy foods or perhaps light, crispy foods?

- Do you ever have these favourite foods now – how often?
- Do you have any bad food memories – foods you were forced to eat or foods you associate with bad times?
- Do you avoid these foods now?

Which foods were considered to be *good* for you? Do you know why?

Thinking about your childhood memories in this way may help you see where some of your ideas about food have come from. These may now form the basis of strongly held values. If the new health messages conflict with these memories you may have difficulty accepting them.

Comfort eating – using food as a treat

Something we learn very quickly as children is to associate food with treats and comfort. Busy parents may say 'Don't bother me now – have a biscuit' or 'Stop crying and you can have a sweet,' 'If you finish it all up you can have some ice-cream.' In every case the child is learning that food can replace love or attention – if only for a short time – or it can be a reward. Later as adults if we are lonely, worried or upset we will turn to food for comfort or treat ourselves to something nice to eat if we want to reward or indulge ourselves. It is often to the same sort of food we were given as children that we turn again as adults for comfort.

Apart from habits we picked up as children and the family traditions we inherited there are many other factors which influence what we choose to eat.

Tick any of these factors you think may affect your choice of food:

- Cost of food
- Advertising
- The food label
- Time to prepare the food
- Time to eat the food
- Appearance
- Smell
- Your cooking skills
- What the family likes/dislikes
- Choice available in the local shops
- How often you go shopping
- Having the kitchen gadgets
- Your mobility
- Your age
- The weather
- Religion/culture
- Traditions
- Taste
- Whether you are alone or not
- Having a freezer/fridge
- What someone else has prepared for you.

Add any more that you can think of.

John provides a good example of how we get set in our ways. John, now aged 50, was a healthy, lean, strong 24-year-old when he started driving a lorry for a living. All those fried breakfasts and meals at transport cafés over the past 26 years, together with little physical activity, has left John four stones overweight with high blood pressure and angina. He now has no choice but to change his habits, as his doctor has told him he needs to lose the four stones in weight. He needs to stop those fried breakfasts and those 'fatty' transport café meals. He needs to look at his whole lifestyle and 'get his house in order' but knowing what to do and being able to do it can sometimes be miles apart.

This chapter will give you the necessary guidance on how to change your lifestyle.

We can now begin to see why it is so hard to change our food habits – they are based on so many different things. Any new way of eating has to fit in with many external factors. It is getting easier for some people to get hold of healthier food. Some of these things you may feel you have no control over, others you could change if you felt it was worthwhile. You can change your habits but you have to really *want to* as it will not be easy. If you are willing to change your eating habits you need to know what to eat.

What do you eat?

Before you can start changing the food you eat, you must first discover *what* it is you eat already.

The only way of doing this is to keep a food diary (see below) for about a week. You not only want to know what you eat but where and when you eat it.

Start your food diary by jotting down everything you have eaten so far today. By the end of the week you will have a clear idea of what your eating habits are. Do not assume you know this already. The food diary may surprise you, as many people are unaware of just how much food and drink they consume between meals.

Food diary – Monday

Time	Food	How much	Place
7.30am	Cornflakes full cream milk sugar Coffee	Large bowl ½ pint 4 teaspoons 2 mugs	Kitchen at home
10.30am	Coffee Doughnut sugar	1 mug One 2 teaspoons	At work sitting at desk
12.30pm	Filled rolls – corned beef/ tomato Crisps	Two 1 packet	At work/office dining room.

When you have completed your food diary, you can then look back and see the amount of unhealthy foods you eat. If you take sugar in your coffee just add up the number of teaspoons of sugar you have taken. You may be surprised. In this way your food diary can be used as you work your way through this chapter. For example, in the **Fibre** section there is a list of changes you can make to increase the fibre content in your diet. Just check your food diary against the list of things to do, you may decide those you are not doing may be worthwhile trying.

Fat

There are two problems with eating too much fat. Firstly, fat is loaded with calories, and too many calories lead to becoming overweight. Secondly, too much *saturated* fat is linked with a higher risk of heart disease. The more saturated fat you eat, the more cholesterol you get in your blood. The cholesterol builds up on the inside of your arteries, especially in the heart. Eventually the arteries can get furred and narrowed which can lead to angina. High cholesterol is perhaps the major cause of *atherosclerosis* (furring up of the arteries with fatty plaques, see Chapter 1).

It is not necessarily the cholesterol in our diet that makes our blood cholesterol high. We only eat approximately 250–500mg of cholesterol per day. Compare this to the amount of fat we eat daily which is approximately 85–100g. We eat at least 200 times as much fat as we do cholesterol. Also there are very few foods which contain significant amounts of cholesterol, these being eggs, offal, shrimps and prawns. It is far more important if you wish to reduce your blood cholesterol to cut down the fat in your diet and not solely concentrate on reducing your dietary cholesterol.

The health message is to cut down on the total amount of fat you eat, and when you do eat fat choose unsaturated fat.

What are the different types of fat?

Firstly, fats and oils are both fats, the difference between them is that fats are solid at room temperature, e.g. butter, and oil is liquid at room temperature, e.g. vegetable oil. Unfortunately, you need to understand much more if you are to know which fat to cut down and what food labels mean.

Fats come in three different types:

- Saturated
- Monounsaturated   } unsaturated
- Polyunsaturated

Saturated and unsaturated fats

These are the two main groups of fats in food. Saturated fats tend to increase the level of cholesterol in our blood and unsaturated fats do not. If anything, they may help to reduce the cholesterol in our blood.

Saturated fats

Saturated fats are found mainly as animal fats in red meats (i.e. beef, lamb and pork, suet, lard, dripping) and dairy products (i.e. milk, cheese and butter). Coconut and palm oil are also saturated vegetable fats. Therefore it is important not to think that all vegetable fats and oils are all right. These types of oils are used extensively in the manufacture of cakes and biscuits.

You also find saturated fats when vegetable oils have been 'hydrogenated'. This means they are artificially made more saturated. Therefore, look out for the label 'hydrogenated vegetable fat'. For example, in the manufacture of margarine, liquid oils are hydrogenated to make them hard enough to spread; thus, the harder the margarine the more saturated the spread.

Unsaturated fats

The following are two types of fat which may actually lower the level of cholesterol in the blood and possibly repair some of the damage done by saturated fats.

Monounsaturated fats – olive oil, peanuts, peanut oil and rape seed oil are rich sources of this type of fat.

Polyunsaturated fats are found in vegetable oils made from seeds and nuts, in special soft margarines labelled 'high in polyunsaturates' and in oily fish such as herring, mackerel and trout.

Summary
Saturates:
- Found in meat, e.g. beef, lamb, pork. Also in suet, lard, dripping and meat products.
- Also in dairy products, e.g. milk, cheese, butter and ghee (used in cooking curries).

- Plus some vegetable fats e.g. coconut and palm oil and in hydrogenated vegetable oil/fat.
- These types of fat are commonly used in biscuits, chocolate, cooking fats, hard margarine, sauces, shop-bought puddings and savoury pastries.
- Increase blood cholesterol.

Polyunsaturates:
- Found in vegetable oil, e.g. sunflower, corn and soya oil.
- In special soft margarines labelled 'high in polyunsaturates', in nuts and all oily fish such as herring, mackerel, pilchards and trout.
- Do not increase blood cholesterol.

Monounsaturates:
- Found in olive oil, peanuts, peanut oil and rape seed oil.
- Do not increase blood cholesterol.

We get too many of our calories from fats; both the American Heart Association[5] and COMA (the Committee on Medical Aspects of Food Policy)[6] in the UK agree we need to reduce the amount of calories from fat, from its present level of approximately 40 per cent to a healthy level of approximately 30 per cent of calories coming from fat and no more than 10 per cent of calories coming from saturated fat.

How do you eat less fat?

You need to discover the main sources of fat in your diet so you can change the foods that really matter. In the average UK diet the fat comes mainly from:

FOOD	STOP AND THINK	GETTING BETTER	IDEAL
CHICKEN and TURKEY	eat less than once a week	eat 1-2 times a week	eat 3 or more times a week
FISH all kinds	eat fish less than once a week	eat fish 1-2 times a week	eat fish 3-4 times a week
RED MEAT Beef, Lamb, Pork, Ham, Bacon	eat red meat 2-3 times a day lean or fatty	eat red meat daily - lean only	eat red meat 2-4 times a week, lean only
MILK	use whole milk	use semi-skimmed milk	use skimmed milk
CHEESE	eat only high fat cheese - Cheddar Stilton Cream Cheese Hard English Cheese Vegetarian Cheese	use a mixture of types of cheese, some low fat	use low fat cheese, cottage cheese, etc. with occasional other types of cheese
CREAM SYNTHETIC CREAM EVAPORATED MILK	use weekly or more often	use less than once a fortnight	use low fat yoghurt, Quark, fromage frais or curd cheese instead of cream or evaporated milk
SPREADS	use butter, ghee or hard margarine	use polyunsaturated margarine	use less than 4oz polyunsaturated margarine a week or low-fat spread
COOKING FATS/OILS	use lard, suet, shortening, coconut, cream or milk, palm oil	use pure vegetable oil	use corn, sunflower or olive oil sparingly
BISCUITS CAKES PASTRY SAVOURIES	eat home-made or bought varieties frequently	eat home-made using polyunsaturated fats only	eat pastry, cakes and biscuits less than 1-2 times a week

Table 5 Towards a lower fat diet

So where do you get most of your fat from?

From the above percentages, you can see over half the fat comes from meat and dairy products and these are saturated fats.

Look at Table 5, 'Towards a Lower Fat Diet'. If you have ticked any boxes in the first column then these are the dietary habits you need to change. Now choose one or two of these dietary habits and try to move them into the middle column. These will be your most important changes. If you have ticked most of the boxes in the middle column, again, pick one/two changes you would like to try to move into the column marked IDEAL.

You are aiming in stages to move slowly towards the IDEAL column. You decide how quickly and how far to go. Do not waste time changing foods you only eat rarely.

Which spread should I use?

Either a high in polyunsaturate spread or a low-fat (high in polyunsaturates) spread. If you need to lose weight then a low-fat (high in polyunsaturates) spread is best for you. In general it is best for everybody to aim for not more than 4oz of spread per week.

Skimmed and semi-skimmed milk contain less fat than ordinary milk. These are good for slimming and reducing fat in the diet. They have just as much calcium and protein as ordinary milk. However, it is advisable not to give skimmed or semi-skimmed milk to babies or children under 5. While milk is still their main food and they rely on it for calories to promote strong and healthy growth, unlike adults who generally eat too many calories.

Cheese

This list gives the fat content of various cheeses.

High fat contains approx 25–40 per cent fat	Medium fat contains approx 20 per cent fat	Low fat contains less than 5 per cent fat
cream cheese	Edam	cottage cheese
Stilton	Gouda	low-fat soft
Danish Blue	Camembert	cheese
Lymeswold	Brie	curd cheese

High fat	Medium fat	Low fat
Cheddar	Babybel	
Leicester	Mozzarella	
Double	Parmesan	
Gloucester	Gruyère	
Cheshire	low-fat cheddars	

When eating cheese it is not just the type of cheese you eat, but also the quantity that matters. If you eat a lot of cheese, i.e. more than 8oz per week, then mainly select cheeses from the low-fat and medium-fat varieties.

What about fibre?

Healthy eating doesn't mean eating less of everything. Fibre is something you can actually eat more of. This will help keep you 'fit on the inside' and protect you from gut disorders like constipation and piles. Foods that are naturally rich in fibre have lots of vitamins and other nutrients too.

Fibre-rich foods

You only get fibre from foods that grow from the ground: cereals, wheat, oats, corn, rice, beans, peas, vegetables and fruit. You don't get any fibre in animal products like cheese, eggs or meat.

You get less fibre if the food has had its outer layer (husk or skin) removed – so peeled potatoes have less fibre than jacket potatoes. White flour has less fibre than wholemeal flour. The word *whole* as in *wholemeal* or *whole grain* will let you know that nothing has been removed.

Fibre and blood cholesterol

Fibre occurs in two forms; soluble and insoluble fibre. It has been found that soluble fibre reduces the amount of cholesterol in your blood. The soluble fibre binds to cholesterol and bile acids (which contain cholesterol) in your gut. Therefore, you do not absorb this cholesterol and as a result your blood cholesterol is reduced.

The following foods are all rich in soluble fibre: beans, all types, e.g. baked, kidney and runner beans; peas, e.g. chick and split; oat bran, porridge and fruit rich in pectin, e.g. apples.

Fibre and weight

Bread and potatoes contain *complex carbohydrate*. This is a starchy food which contains natural fibre. In the past bread and potatoes were considered along with *refined carbohydrate* (starchy food which contains no fibre e.g. sugar, plain biscuits) as food which makes you put weight on. But we now know that the bulky *complex carbohydrates*, e.g. potatoes, wholemeal bread and brown rice, are just the foods which help us stay slim and healthy because these foods fill us up without overloading us with calories.

A small bar of milk chocolate (60g/2oz) contains approximately 320 calories. This is equivalent to 400g/14oz of boiled potatoes (eight egg-sized potatoes). Which of these would fill you up the most?

Some ways to eat more fibre

Tick the things you already do. Put a tick by the tips you think you could try, then just change one new thing per week. The more tips you tick, the higher your diet will be in fibre.

Tips

- Try to eat at least four slices of bread a day. Wholemeal bread is best but all bread is good food. Chapatis and pitta bread are good for fibre, especially as they are made from wholemeal flour.
- Use wholemeal flour instead of white flour for baking – mixtures of the flours work well in most recipes – try half wholemeal and half white.
- Breakfast cereals can be great for fibre – go for ones with ingredients that are wholegrains and avoid sugar-coated types.
- Try using more peas, beans and lentils. In many meals you can replace some or all of the meat with beans – much cheaper and still very good food.
- Eat more potatoes, also cassava, plantain and yams.
- Brown rice has more fibre than white. It takes longer to cook, but it is very tasty.
- Eat more unsalted nuts and dried fruit – perhaps instead of confectionery.
- Try to eat at least one piece of fruit a day and get a good variety

of vegetables. Some are better than others but they all have some fibre and plenty of essential vitamins and minerals.

Sugar

In Britain on average we buy almost one pound of sugar per week per adult. We actually eat almost double this amount as there is so much sugar present in other foods we buy, e.g. sweets, soft drinks, biscuits, cakes, soups, sauces etc.

There are two main problems with eating too much sugar. Firstly, sugar promotes tooth decay, especially when you have sugary snacks and drinks frequently throughout the day. Secondly, sugar promotes obesity. Adding sugar to foods makes it easier for us to eat too much – and take in too many calories.

Sugar and blood cholesterol

Sugar does not directly increase blood cholesterol levels, but if you are overweight this can increase your cholesterol level. This does not necessarily mean if you are not overweight you can eat as much sugar as you wish. Sugar contains only calories and very little goodness in terms of vitamins and minerals.

Sucrose, glucose, dextrose, fructose, maltose, syrup, raw sugar, brown sugar, cane sugar, honey, muscovado, and molasses are all sugar.

We do not need sugar for energy – we get energy from all the foods we eat

Look back at your list of favourite childhood foods (see page 167). Count how many of them are sweet. If most of your favourites were sweet then the chances are that you still eat a lot of sweet foods now. Why do you think this is? Do we all naturally love sweetness? Are we 'born with a sweet tooth'? – or does it link back with treats and bribes you were given as a child? Were your taste buds trained to crave for sugary foods just through habit?

Many dentists and dietitians bring their children up to eat as little sugar as possible. As a result many of these children reach adulthood with absolutely no tooth fillings. Do you think this is extreme, or sensible? It is certainly not easy as there is so much sugar around.

Ways of cutting down sugar

Tick the things you already do. Put a * by the tips you could try. Just change one new strategy per week.

- Try drinking your tea or coffee without sugar. You might find it easier to cut down a little at a time. Using an artificial sweetener gets rid of the sugar but not your desire for the sweet taste.
- When buying soft drinks, choose low-calorie ones or unsweetened fruit juice.
- Buy tinned fruit in natural juice rather than syrup.
- Look at the ingredients in breakfast cereals and avoid those with added sugar (some of the sugar-coated varieties are 50 per cent sugar!)
- Use fresh fruit or unsalted nuts as snacks instead of sweets or chocolate.
- Go easy on cakes and biscuits. They can add a lot of sugar and fat to your diet.
- Sugar substitutes can be used if you find it difficult to give up the sweet taste of foods. They contain hardly any calories and do not rot your teeth.

Alcohol and blood cholesterol

Alcohol has not been proven to be protective against coronary heart disease. Its effect on blood cholesterol levels is similar to that of sugar. Alcohol does not directly increase blood cholesterol levels, but too much can lead to obesity which in turn tends to increase blood cholesterol levels.

Alcohol is often talked about in terms of standard drinks or units. A unit is equivalent to 10g of alcohol:

1 pint of beer/lager = 2 units
1 glass wine   = 1 unit
1 glass spirit   = 1 unit
(standard measure)

A sensible limit for alcohol for men is between 4 and 6 units two or three times per week and for women 2–3 units two or three times per week.

Below is a brief list of alcoholic drinks and their calorie content.

Type	Calories per 100 ml	Calories per serving	Measure
Beer			
Ale/dark beer	32	106	330ml/½ pint
Lager	29	87	330ml/½ pint
Cider			
Dry	36	108	330ml/½ pint
Sweet	42	126	330ml/½ pint
Vintage	101	303	330ml/½ pint
Wine			
Red	68	102	150 ml glass
Dry white	66	99	150ml glass
Medium white	75	113	150ml glass
Sweet white	94	141	150ml glass
Port	157	78	50ml/⅓ gill
Sherry			
Dry	116	58	50ml/⅓ gill
Sweet	136	68	50ml/⅓ gill
Spirits			
70% proof	222	56	25ml/⅙ gill

Salt

On average we eat about 10 grams of salt a day, that is two whole
teaspoons. Much of this is contained in processed foods such as
cheese, cakes, cereals, biscuits and savoury snacks. Everyone
needs some salt but most people do not need more than 1 gram
per day.

   For some people, eating too much salt can lead to high blood
pressure and for those people with high blood pressure already,
reducing the amount of salt you eat could help bring it down. At
the moment there is no way of knowing in advance who are likely
to be responsive to salt in this way.

   If you want to play safe, cut down on the amount of salt you
eat. If you do suffer from high blood pressure, then your doctor
will be monitoring it, but you can also see if reducing your salt
intake reduces your blood pressure.

Ways of cutting down salt

Tick the things you already do, put a * by the tips you could try.
Just change one new item per week. The more tips you achieve,
the lower in salt your diet will be.

- Use less salt in cooking.
- Use pepper, vinegar, spices, lemon juice or mustard to add flavour to your food.
- Get out of the habit of adding salt to food at the table. Always taste your food prior to adding salt. Think before you shake!
- Cut down on salty snack foods like crisps, salted nuts and other savoury nibbles.
- If you buy tinned vegetables buy those marked 'No added salt'.
- Use fewer tinned and packet soups, as these can be high in salt – why not make you own?
- Cut down on salted meats such as bacon, gammon and salt beef.

Sea salt and ordinary salt are virtually identical. Sea salt contains traces of minerals, otherwise it is the same and has the same effect on blood pressure.

Salt substitutes are better than ordinary salt. They tend to be high in potassium. This is good for most people, but if you have a kidney or heart condition it is recommended that you check with your doctor before use.

Obesity

First, being overweight places more stress on the heart, which is not a good idea if you suffer from angina. Second, if you are overweight you stimulate cholesterol production and therefore your blood cholesterol levels tend to be higher, also not a good idea.

If you do need to lose weight:

- don't bother about calorie counting – this is too complicated.
- eat plenty of vegetables, fruit and wholegrain foods.
- cut down on fats and sugars
- take regular exercise (see Chapter 8 on exercise). You will burn off calories doing the exercise but, more importantly, you reset your 'ticking over rate' and generally burn up more calories throughout the day. It takes more calories to keep a fit body ticking over. Hence, the fitter the body, the easier it is to lose weight.

● only weigh yourself once a week, preferably at the same time each week and on the same scales. Aim for an average weight loss of 1–2 lbs (0.5–1 kg) each week.

If you find it difficult to cut out certain foods here are a few tips that may help you:

● Eat slowly – this makes meals last longer and you may feel fuller.
● Reduce tempting situations for food and eating.
● Only keep food in the kitchen or pantry.
● Keep food away from the table. Do not put a whole loaf of bread on the table, just the slices you wish to eat.
● Avoid passing by a particular shop if you are likely to see foods that may tempt you.
● Remember, if you don't buy the food and it is not in the house you can't eat it.
● Only eat at the kitchen/dining table, not directly from the fridge or cupboards.
● Try not to eat when you are doing other things, e.g. watching television or reading.
● Have regular meals, particularly breakfast and do not skip meals or you may get too hungry and binge.
● Have a stock of low-calorie and healthy, filling foods such as fruit and fresh vegetables to hand if you get hungry. It is better than bingeing on cakes or ice cream.

It is not easy to lose weight. The most important thing is not to go on any crash diets but to adjust to a healthy lifestyle and watch your weight come down gradually.

But how do I change my diet?

You may find that in order to improve your diet you will need to change the eating habits of the people who live with you. To succeed, everyone will need to be involved in making the decisions and everyone will need to be motivated. Probably the best way of tackling the problem is for you all to work through the chapter and then compare the answers you have all given. This way you can come up with a 'house plan'. Alternatively, they can suggest changes they might like to try from the list of good eating tactics in order to improve their diet.

Remember that any changes you decide to make will have to be practical and right for your circumstances if they are going to last.

It is advisable to make a few dietary changes which you can stick to for life, rather than making several dietary changes for a few months, which then become a chore so the whole new diet is then in danger of being abandoned.

A solution would not be, in the case of a busy family, all to decide to have different evening meals. Even if everyone was prepared to do their own cooking, it would get very expensive and very messy in the kitchen! You may also be more tempted to snack if you see another person eating, even if you only sit down for a chat, having eaten earlier.

Summary

Now that you have read through the chapter, you will be aware of the key factors in the diet concerned with Coronary Heart Disease for people wishing to prevent the disease and for those already suffering with the disease.

The key factors are fats, in particular the type of fat and the quantity. You should be eating less total fat in your diet and slightly increasing the proportion of unsaturated vegetable fats. You should not be overweight, and if you are, you should do something about it. You need to eat more fibre, preferably soluble fibre (fibre from beans, lentils and pulses/legumes). For those people suffering from high blood pressure, reducing your salt intake may help. The most important strategy concerning any dietary change is: it must be enjoyable, and therefore become part of your everyday lifestyle.

Bon appétit!

CHAPTER 11

Angina and self-help

This chapter concerns the main points of beginning and maintaining a support group. It gives you advice on how to select group leaders and gives a description of the key workers within the group. It covers the role of professional involvement and suggests why you should involve these people in the group. The experiences of the South Birmingham Angina Group, which has been running for three years, is discussed, its successes and failures, its aims and objectives, and a typical year in the Group's life is charted. Finally, in the Further Information section on page 204, you will find a list of useful addresses of similar or related groups.

As discussed in Chapter 5, social support can act as a buffer to stress. Self-help groups are one form of this buffer. They allow people who are experiencing the disease to support others who might be newly diagnosed, or who might be experiencing greater difficulties. Another important function of a support group is that the members can concentrate on the things that they *can* do as opposed to the things that they *can't* do. Support groups have proved popular for a number of health conditions and are at last being recognized by doctors as a necessary part of the complete management of an illness. Last, but not least, a theme which is emphasized throughout this book is that of the patient taking an active interest in the management of her/his condition. Support groups promote this sense of responsibility and self-reliance.

The following guidelines are based on three years' experience of running a support group for patients with chronic stable angina, and hopefully will encourage more people to participate in a support group.

However, all support groups will be different because the

people within them will be different, and each of the suggestions will have to be adapted to fit the group that you may be a member of.

Caution – group organizers at work!

One of the most important points about starting a support group of any kind, but particularly an angina support group, is to make sure that you, the organizers, have support! Having angina often means having to accept that you will have days where energy levels are low, so it is important to plan for these days and therefore reduce the frustration that this brings. If you intend to begin a support group, this will have to be considered and allowed for.

Forming a support group is tiring, often frustrating, sometimes hard work and time-consuming, but can be fun, very rewarding and gives some people a new lease of life. The advantages have to be weighed against the disadvantages before you begin; otherwise, if the group does not function well, the participants will experience having their hopes and expectations raised and then dashed and the organizers will experience a sense of failure.

Beginning a group

The first step is to do some **market research.** Find out whether there will be enough interested people living in your area. This can be done by going along to your cardiologist's outpatient clinic and asking the people who attend. Alternatively, you could ask your GP to put you in touch with other people on her/his list who have angina, or put a simple notice in the waiting room of your local surgery or in your local newspaper. Remember, at this stage you are just trying to find out how many people with angina want a group and how many would help to organize one.

Once you have ascertained there is a need for your group, then you can think about some practical arrangements. If you have not already done so, approach your cardiologist, discuss your ideas with her/him and solicit her/his support. More about this last point in the section on involving professionals on page 189.

Money

You will need some financial assistance for this project. Obviously, the more the better, but you can begin with just enough to pay for a room to be hired and to cover the costs of your attenders' refreshments. Go to your local library and ask for the Charities' Handbook. This is a list of all the registered charities in Britain, some of whom will donate small sums of money to getting a group started. (In other countries, ask your local library for a list of charities.)

Once you have a list of the appropriate charities, cost out your application for grant aid. Some useful things to consider are:

a) The cost of room per meeting,
b) Refreshments,
c) Publicity materials,
d) Organizers' costs (telephone bills, stamps, letter paper, etc.),
e) Payment for speakers for the year,
f) Any necessary equipment purchase.

Most starter grants will cover these costs. However, you may wish to be a bit more ambitious and ask for writing materials, a typewriter, tape recorder or video recording machine to educate your participants. You may not get what you ask for but you may get some help towards the total cost.

It is advisable right from the very beginning to keep meticulous accounts. This will ensure that your sponsors are aware of where their money is being spent and it will help in the future running of the group and reapplication for grants.

Once you have been given a sum of money to start a group, you need to enlist the help of at least one other person and open an account to hold the money. Then begin to concentrate on advertising your group.

Going public

The first step is to let people know you exist. Contact local GPs, your cardiologist, local hospital coronary care units, other coronary support groups, put up notices in local shops and in your local newspaper. Maybe even contact local radio and/or television stations and ask if they are interested in doing an article on your group. When advertising yourself, bear in mind the following points:

a) Let people know the name of your group – avoid names such as 'The Victims of . . .', '. . . Sufferers' or '. . . Cripples'. Consider – would you want to join a group which suggested hopelessness or inferiority? Be positive.
b) Give people the name of someone to contact and an address or telephone number – consider whether this contact person should be you. Bear in mind that you might be inundated with requests for information.
c) Make explicit the aim of your group – keep this simple, perhaps along the lines of 'to offer support and education to people with angina about angina'.
d) Make it clear who the group is for, i.e. all people with heart disease? People with angina only? Families of people with angina?
e) Make your advertisement eye-catching, light and even amusing, but most of all make your main message **clear** and **precise**.

Getting started

Once you have a handful of people interested in attending and helping to organize the group, then you have started. The next stage is to call a meeting to identify **key roles** and elect members to those roles. The first 'official' meeting should have an agenda and someone to record the decisions you have made. You can do this is an informal way but still get the 'business' achieved. Some items which should be included for discussion and decisions recorded on are:

a) The 'official' aim(s) of the group,
b) The key members' roles,
c) The activities for the forthcoming year,
d) How recruitment will be achieved.

It is possible for just a couple of people to run a support group but this can place undue stress on those members and for many reasons forming a committee is preferable. This committee will enable decisions to be made democratically and the burden of decision-making is thus shared. There are a number of essential committee members for good running of a support group. These are:

a) **The co-ordinator** – someone who oversees others and is the communication link between the other members. This person should be calm, confident and articulate as she/he will often be asked to act as the main spokesperson for the group.

b) **The secretary** – someone who is able to record accurately the points that have been raised in meetings, the decisions that have been made, communicating those decisions to all members in a clear and precise way. This job would be better done by someone who has access to a typewriter or word processor and can type!

c) **The treasurer** – someone who can keep accurate accounts of any money coming in and going out. Preferably someone with experience in book-keeping, but this is not absolutely necessary.

d) **A publicity officer** – This person will be responsible for advertising the group, designing a diary which shows the forthcoming events, and recruiting new members.

These are the essential roles but there will be many more to consider depending on your type of group. One other you may want to consider is that of fund-raiser – this can often be time-consuming and stressful so if it can be shared it will lighten the load. To some extent the size of the group will determine the number of people running it but the fewer tasks each person has to perform, the more energy they will have for enjoying the group's activities.

Maintaining a group

The initial enthusiasm and commitment to the group will help you through beginning the group. Maintaining that level of enthusiasm has to be carefully managed. One of the most important ways you can maintain this momentum is to find out how often the group needs to meet. The optimum frequency seems to be about once a month, but some groups prefer to meet more frequently, some less. It is important that the committee meets separately to discuss any business and to support each other. This need not be more frequently than every month.

One of the ways to encourage people to attend is to introduce speakers, professionals or experts, to talk about aspects of angina. Alternating a speaker with an open meeting so that members can exchange ideas seems to be a good combination. It is important to plan ahead so that all members know what event is happening and when. It is important also to have a fixed meeting time and date. If the time and/or date of the meeting changes, people simply forget it. So, having a regular time, e.g. last Tuesday in every month, and a regular time of day of the beginning *and* the end of a meeting, will help people remember.

Advertising and recruitment will need to be continued even though the group has started. You may find that a regular core of people make up the group but others will come and go having given or got what they wanted from the group. If you find a large number of people only come once, then perhaps you need to examine whether the group is doing what it set out to do. However, if a small number of people come for a short time only but appear to be happy with the group, perhaps they only had to attend for a few sessions to get what they needed.

Remember to keep up the publicity – keeping a moderately high profile will encourage new members, possibly attract sources of income and boost the morale of the existing members. This last point should never be overlooked.

What makes good group leaders?

There is much written about what makes good leaders generally but there is no doubt that two qualities in particular are essential for any type of self-help group. One is enthusiasm and the other is commitment to the aims of the group. Enthusiasm does not mean boundless energy which drains everyone who witnesses it, but a quiet persistence, a positive attitude and an encouraging nature. This is the person who will attract group members, some of whom will want to become actively involved in running the group. Commitment, on the other hand, implies a willingness to learn, sometimes by making mistakes, a desire to do what is best for the group (not just for themselves) and a strong belief in the group's function.

A good group leader will be someone who can communicate well with all members and sometimes clear up miscommunications. This requires a relaxed, warm approach even to the most difficult members. Communication is the hub of co-ordination. It can involve facilitating communication between other organizers, between organizers and ordinary members, between oneself and the group and between the group and others in the community. These are important roles of the nominated leader/ co-ordinator.

Another skill that a good co-ordinator needs is an ability to pass on their skills learned through experiences of the group to other, future leaders. A group leader who cannot let go of the role is a drain on the group's resources. Training the incoming group co-ordinator should be made explicitly part of the co-ordinator's role. This can be achieved by the new leader overlapping with the outgoing leader for a time to see how the job is done. This staggering of positions could also be done with the other key roles.

Finally, the ability to make executive decisions, as and when necessary, should not be underestimated. This does not mean a domineering megalomaniac, but someone who knows when a decision has to be made by them, does so, and accepts the consequences of doing so.

Obviously, training for group leaders would seem to be an ideal thing but training can be costly, even if one could find an appropriate training course, although there might be one available at a further education college. This is not essential, however, and many untrained people who are simply open to suggestion about their style of leadership and who are sensitive to other people's needs and feelings make excellent group leaders.

Involving professional people

There is little doubt that involving professionals in the running of a support group is useful. Having professional people involved can give the group a higher profile and status in the eyes of people with angina and in those of the people involved in making decisions about giving grant aid. They may act as links with speakers you may wish to involve in the group and they may offer essential advice on topics that members will be asking questions about, for example, diet, exercise, medication and stress.

The key professional to involve in an angina support group is a sympathetic cardiologist. He/she may act as a recruitment agent for new members, may offer his/her skills by educating the group about their angina, and also may have access to other professionals and/or organizations the group may want to use.

If there is a psychologist available, he/she can also provide expertise on stress management, stopping smoking, training group organizers, individual therapy or counselling for those who may require it and can provide links with other professionals.

The third person it is helpful to involve is a physiotherapist, preferably one who has experience of cardiac rehabilitation. He/she can provide information on exercise and enhancing the self-management of fitness and angina in a safe and enjoyable way.

You might want to think about involving a dietitian, who can give advice on healthy eating, diet for reducing weight or high cholesterol. You may also want to involve a social worker or rehabilitation counsellor to advice on disability benefits or re-employment opportunities.

The extent to which you involve these other people will be a personal decision, but the main reason for doing so will be to help you build on your skills to manage your angina safely and expertly, thereby enhancing your quality of life.

There are many professional charity workers or voluntary body co-ordinators who will be happy to be consulted about organizing and co-ordinating (e.g. National Council of Voluntary Organizations in London). Keeping a list of key people in the relevant organizations which, in Britain, include the Chest, Heart and Stroke Association and British Heart Foundation, is recommended. These people have access to nationwide communication networks which your organization can both contribute to and benefit from.

The South Birmingham Angina Support Group

This began as a result of a unique research programme which

Fig 30

involves psychology, cardiology, and physiotherapy in the management of chronic stable angina. It grew out of a few interested people meeting to encourage each other to practise the relaxation training they had been taught by the psychologist involved in the research.

The research promoted stress management training which involved self-management of angina through relaxation training, thought and behaviour control and understanding the importance of emotions, especially anger, in angina. This was usually done in seven sessions of 1½ hours per week, with a follow-up session which was designed to reinforce the training occurring about two months after the last session. The stress management trainees saw this final session as having a dual purpose, to reinforce the previous learning and to provide ongoing support for the members. The need for a more structured approach to supporting the group members and an ongoing education programme about angina soon became apparent and in 1986 the Angina Self-Help Group was formed.

The main organizers in the early stage included the research psychologist and a couple of the people with angina who had been through the research programme. The Group was awarded a starter grant of £200 and a room was found to hold regular, monthly meetings. As new members came through from the ongoing research project a committee was formed and the programme of events for the forthcoming year was planned. The first task the group as a whole performed together was to design a logo to help advertise the Group.

The group's main aims were a) to provide a forum for people with angina to meet and discuss issues related to the management of their condition, b) to provide opportunities for people with angina, and their partners, to learn more about the management of angina by talks/presentations from visiting experts.

The Group advertised its presence in the local paper and received many enquiries and a number of new recruits from the exercise. As the Group began to expand, some questions regarding its aims arose. Should partners be invited to the meetings? Should the group be expanded to include people with heart disease other than angina? At this point, over a year into the venture, another meeting was called to discuss these issues and to elect a new committee.

At first the Group members were reluctant to offer themselves as organizers, but with some explanation about the roles and assurance that responsibilities would be shared, a new committee was formed. A few key members, who had been part of the committee the previous year, remained to help the newer members. The Group adopted the simpler, more descriptive title of Angina Support Group.

This annual meeting was useful, not just to elect new members to the organizers' committee, but to reevaluate the Group's aims and restate its objectives. The group organizers made contact with the organizers from a similar cardiac group from another area. This group had been established for some time and included people with a range of heart problems and met regularly. Many useful ideas and experiences were exchanged and it proved to be a very useful contact. The organizers were able to talk about the group and its aims to the Angina Support Group and links with other groups were also planned.

A typical year of South Birmingham's Angina Support Group

The Group had decided to meet monthly for one hour at a regular time and place. The meetings were organized to alternate a speaker with an open meeting. The point of the open meeting was to have an opportunity to discuss any issues that had been raised by the speaker's talk and to have time and place to perform relaxation.

The psychologist acted as a contact for the key speakers and liaised between them and the Support Group. Suggestions about who the Group wanted as speakers came from the members themselves and all suggestions were considered, not just those from prominent members.

January
A social welfare officer discussed the social services definition of disability and introduced the members to the entitlements and state benefits they would be entitled to if classified disabled.

February
An open meeting, where members socialized and welcomed any new members, was followed by a short session of relaxation for those who wanted it.

March
A representative from the cardiology team talked about medical aspects of managing angina, including drug treatment and coronary artery bypass surgery.

April
The open meeting continued discussion of the issues raised by the medical talk on angina. This was followed by a relaxation session.

May
The psychologist presented the results from the pilot study of the research in which the members had participated.

June
The June meeting was organized as a social event. All members were asked to contribute to the organization. Some baked cakes, some supplied sandwiches, quiches, or other savoury dishes. Music was supplied by a member's daughter and the support group themselves provided the conversation.

July
The physiotherapist who was involved with the research talked about exercise and angina.

August
This open meeting was again used as an opportunity to meet and welcome new members and to discuss the previous month's talk. A session of relaxation was conducted at the end of the meeting following a brief business meeting to discuss any issues raised from the previous six months.

September
A dietitian talked about diet and angina, and in particular the role of cholesterol in heart disease.

October
During this meeting videos discussing the effects of heart attacks on angina and sexual functioning were shown. These had been supplied, free of charge, by the Chest, Heart and Stroke Association.

November
A representative from the Chest, Heart and Stroke Association had been invited to talk about the work of the organization.

December

This meeting centred on a Christmas celebration organized along the lines of the June social event where members socialized and met any new members who had joined.

January

This opportunity was taken to combine a business meeting, discussion of accounts and reselection of new committee members, with planning the forthcoming year's events.

Although the organization of the monthly meetings was not as uncomplicated as it first appears, generally it was trouble-free. However, one meeting which had been scheduled had to be reorganized because the speaker did not turn up. It is useful to have something in reserve for occasions like this and the use of video playback facilities at short notice can be useful. Many of the main charities will supply health education videos which can be used to stimulate discussion. Alternatively, a list of discussion topics can be generated and one of the group members can lead discussion on an appropriate topic.

The South Birmingham Angina Support Group has been very lucky in having a room and relaxation equipment, pillows and mats, available to them free of charge. Fortunately, speakers to date have not asked for a fee and the venue is easily accessible to most of the group members. All these factors have undoubtedly helped in the smooth running of the Support Group. However, without the persistent enthusiasm and excellent organization skills of a few key members the Group would not exist and it must be recognized that the maxim 'where there's a will, there's a way' is certainly the unofficial motto of the South Birmingham Angina Support Group.

Glossary

Aerobic: in the presence of oxygen

Age Predicted Maximum Heart Rate: an estimate of the maximum number of heartbeats your heart can manage in one minute for your age using the formula 220 minus age

Anaerobic: in the absence of oxygen

Angiography (angiogram or arteriogram): a special X-ray picture of the heart which involves injecting radio-opaque dye into the coronary arteries and which can be seen on a special screen

Angioplasty: opening a narrowed coronary artery by expanding a 'balloon' within it

Anterior Descending Artery: a branch of the main left coronary artery

Atheroma: small fatty deposits which line the artery walls in coronary disease

Atherosclerosis: the name for the thickening and hardening process which occurs with atheroma in coronary disease

Beta-blocker (ß-blocker): a drug which reduces the workload on the heart over a long period of time and therefore reduces the number of angina attacks occurring

CAD: Coronary Artery Disease (see also IHD)

Cardiac Output: the volume of blood pumped out of the heart, usually in terms of litres per minute

Cardiologist: heart specialist

Carotid Artery: major artery situated in the neck which supplies blood to the head and neck

Cholesterol: part of the body structure and a normal constituent of the blood. Most adults contain approximately 140 grams (5 oz). It is needed for cell membranes, particularly nerves. A raised blood cholesterol is an important risk factor in heart disease

Circumflex Artery: a branch of the main left coronary artery

Collateral System: a small network of tiny arteries which connects the coronary arteries

Complex Carbohydrate: starchy food that has not had the fibre removed, e.g. wholemeal flour and wholemeal breakfast cereals

Coronary Arteries: one of the two main arteries which supply the heart with oxygen

Coronary Artery Bypass Graft (CABG): operation to bypass a narrowed coronary artery

Coronary Care Unit: a specialized hospital ward which exclusively treats people with heart conditions

Coronary Spasm: small twitching movements in the coronary arteries which temporarily interrupt the essential blood supply

Coronary Thrombosis: a blood or atheroma clot which blocks off an artery

Diabetes: a disease of the pancreas gland which upsets the production of insulin, resulting in poor metabolism of sugar

Dietary Fibre: part of the diet we cannot digest

ECG: a heart tracing which is obtained by electrodes placed on the chest that convert a signal from the heart to a visual pattern

Electrocardiograph: ECG

Exercise Tolerance Testing (ETT or treadmill test): exercising the heart under controlled conditions to look for the ECG changes associated with angina

Gastroscopy (Endoscopy): a 'telescope' examination of the oesophagus and stomach to look for ulcers

Glyceryl Trinitrate (GTN): a drug which reduces the workload of the heart acutely and therefore relieves (or prevents) an attack of angina

IHD: Ischaemic Heart Disease (see also CAD)

Insoluble Fibre: a component of dietary fibre which does not necessarily reduce blood cholesterol but helps prevent constipation. Found in whole products, also in fruit and vegetables

Isometric Exercise: exercise where the muscles work hard against a load but there is no change in the length of the muscle

Isotonic Exercise: exercise including free rhythmic movement, where the muscles shorten and lengthen as they work

Lactic Acid: substance produced by the body during anaerobic metabolism

Maximal Oxygen Uptake: the largest volume of oxygen extracted from inspired air by the body during physical work

Menopause: the change that occurs in the production of the female hormones progesterone and oestrogen after middle age in women

Monounsaturated fats: these are fatty acids with one double bond in them, mainly found in vegetables. They do not increase the blood cholesterol

Myocardial Ischaemia: evidence on investigation that the heart muscle is deficient in blood and therefore oxygen

Myocarditis: inflammation of the myocardium or heart muscle

Myocardium: the name of the muscle layer of the heart

Natural pacemaker: a bundle of special nerve fibres in the heart which receive signals that regulate the heart rhythm

Oestrogen: one of the two main reproductive hormones in women

Osteoporosis: a condition where there is loss of bone density and reduction in thickness of the outer layer of the bone

Oxygen Demand: the amount of oxygen the heart requires to perform the job of beating adequately

Polyunsaturated fats: these are fatty acids with two or more double bonds in them, mainly found in vegetables and fish. They do not increase blood cholesterol

Progesterone: one of the two main reproductive hormones in women

Radial Artery: artery situated in the arm which is easily felt at the wrist and which is commonly used for taking the pulse or the number of heartbeats per minute

Refined Carbohydrate: starchy food that has had the fibre removed, e.g. sugar

Risk Factor: a potential cause of a heart attack or coronary disease

Saturated fats: these are fatty acids with no double bonds in them. They are mainly found in animal fats and they increase the level of blood cholesterol

Silent Ischaemia: evidence of an interrupted blood supply to the heart but without accompanying angina

Silent Myocardial Infarction: evidence on examination of a healed heart attack which the person concerned was not aware of occurring

Soluble Fibre: a component of dietary fibre which reduces blood cholesterol, found in oats, beans, lentils, fruit rich in pectin, and vegetables

Stroke: the result of an event (such as rupture or blockage) which occurs in the arteries surrounding the brain (cerebral arteries)

Thallium scan: scan demonstrating the pattern of blood supply to the heart muscle

References and further reading

Introduction

1. Ornish, D., Scherwitz, Doody, R.S., et al, 'Effects of Stress Management Training and Dietary Changes in Treating Ischemic Heart Disease.' *Journal of the American Medical Association*, 249 (1) (1983), pp 54–9.
2. Wallace, L., Bundy, C., 'Stress Management Training in the treatment of patients with chronic stable angina.' in West & Spinks (eds) *Clinical psychology in action: A collection of case studies* (John Wright & Sons Ltd, London, 1986).
3. Bundy, E.C., Wallace, L.M., Nagle, R.E., 'Stress Management Training in Chronic Stable Angina'. *International Journal of Psychology and Health* (in press).

Chapter 1

References

1. Jenkins, C.D., 'Recent Evidence Supporting Psychologic and Social Risk Factors for Coronary Disease'. *N Eng J Med*, 294, 1033–1038, (1976).
2. Medalie, J.H., Synder, M., Groen, J.J., *et al*, 'Angina Pectoris Among 10,000 Men: Five Year Incidence and Univariate Analysis', *Am J Med*, 55, 583–594, (1973).
3. Sales, S.M., 'Organisational Role as a Risk Factor in Coronary Disease', *Admin Sci*, 14, 325–336, (1969).
4. Parkes, C.M., Benjamin, B., Fitzgerald, R.G., 'Broken Heart: a Statistical Study of Increased Mortality Among Widowers, *BMJ*, 1, 740–3, (1969).
5. Cooper, T. and The Review Panel on Coronary Prone Behaviour and Coronary Heart Disease, 'Coronary Prone Behaviour and

Coronary Heart Disease: a Critical Review', *Circulation*, *63*, 1199–1215, (1981).
6. Deanfield, J.E., Shea, M.J., Kensett, M., *et al*, 'Silent Myocardial Ischaemia due to Mental Stress', *Lancet, I*, 1001–1005, (1974).
7. Fox, K.M., 'Silent Ischaemia: Clinical Implications in 1988', *Br. Heart J, 60*, 363–6, (1988).

Further reading

Alpert, J.S., *The Heart Attack Handbook* (2nd edition). (Little, Brown & Co., Boston, USA, 1985).
Phibbs, B., *The Human Heart: A Consumer's Guide to Coronary Care*. (The C.V. Mosby Co., St Louis, USA, 1982).

Chapter 2

Further reading

G. Jackson, *The Practical Management of Ischaemic Heart Disease*. (Martin Dunitz, London, 1988).
D.L.H. Patterson, *The Management of Angina Pectoris*. (Castle House Publications Ltd, Tunbridge Wells, 1987).
J.P. Shillingford, *Coronary Heart Disease. The Facts*. (Oxford University Press, Oxford, 1981).

Chapter 3

References

1. Frankenhauser, M., et al, 'Psychobiological aspects of life stress', in Levine, H. and Ursin, S. (ed), *Coping and Health*, (Plenum, New York, 1980).
2. Sutherland, V. and Cooper, C.L., *Man and Accidents Offshore*. (Lloyds of London Press, London, 1986).
3. Lazarus, R.S., *Patterns of Adjustment*. (McGraw-Hill, New York, 1976).
4. Maslach, C. and Pines, A., 'Burnout: the loss of human caring', in *Experiencing Social Psychology*, edited by C. Maslach. (Random House, New York, 1979).
5. Meichenbaum, D., *Stress Inoculation Training*. (John Wiley, New York, 1983).
6. Selye, H., *Stress in Health and Disease*. (Butterworth, London, 1986).

Further reading

Cox, T., *Stress*. (Macmillan, London, 1978).

Powell, K., *Fight Stress and Win!* (Thorsons, Wellingborough, 1988).

Rudinger, E. (ed), *Understanding Stress*. (Consumers Association, UK, 1988).

Chapter 4

References

1. Holmes, T.H., Rahe, R.H., 'The Social Readjustment Rating Scale', *Journal of Psychosomatic Research*, 1967, II, 213–218.
2. Kanner, A.D. et al, 'Daily Hassles', *Journal of Behavioural Medicine*, 4, (1981).
3. Marshall, J. and Cooper, C.L., *Executives Under Pressure*. (Macmillan, London, 1979).
4. Wyler, A.R., Holmes, T.H. and Masuda, M., 'Magnitude of Life Events and Seriousness of Illness', *Psychosomatic Medicine*, 33, 115–22 (1971).

Further reading

Albrecht, K., *Stress and the Manager: Making it work for you*, (Prentice-Hall, New Jersey, 1979).

Cooper, C.L., Cooper, R.D., and Eaker, L.H., *Living with Stress*, (Penguin, Harmondsworth, 1988).

Handy, C., *Understanding Organisations*. (Penguin, Harmondsworth, 1976).

International Labour Office, *Introducing Work Study*, 1974.

Lakein, A., *How to get control of your time and your life*. (Wyden, New York, 1973).

Wilson, K. and Hunt, E., *How to survive the 9 to 5*. (Thames/Methuen, 1986).

Chapter 5

References

1. Derogatis, L., 'The Derogatis Stress Profile', *Journal of Psychosomatic Research*, 30, I, 77–91.
2. Friedman, M.D., and Rosenman, R.H., *Type A Behaviour and Your Heart*, (Knopf, New York, 1974).
3. Barefoot, J.C., Dahlstron, G. and Williams, R.B., 'Hostility, CHD incidence and total mortality: A 25 year follow-up study of 255 physicians', *Psychosomatic Medicine*, 45, I.

4. Williams, R.B., Haney, T.L., Lee, K.L., et al, 'Type A Behaviour, hostility and coronary atherosclerosis', *Psychosomatic Medicine*, 42, 6, (1980).
5. Novaco, R.W., 'The cognitive regulation of anger and stress'. In Kendall, P., and Hallon, S. (eds), *Cognitive behavioural interventions: theory and procedures*, (Academic Press, New York, 1979).
6. Kobasa, S.E., 'Stressful life events, personality and health: an inquiry into hardiness', *Journal of Personality and Social Psychology*, 27, 1-11, (1979).

Further reading

Alberti, R.D. and Emmons, M.L., *Your Perfect Right: A Guide to Assertive Behaviour*, (Impact, New York, 1970).
Marsh, P. (ed), *Eye to Eye: How People Interact*, (Salem House, Massachussets, 1988).
Shaffer, M., *Life After Stress*, (Contemporary Books, Chicago, 1983).
Steiner, C., *Scripts People Live By*, (Grove Press, 1974).
Wood, C., *Living in Overdrive*, (Fontana, 1984).

Chapter 6

References

1. Lee, J.A., 'The Role of the Sympathetic Nervous System in Ischaemic Heart Disease: a Review of the Epidemiological Features and Risk Factors, Integration with Clinical and Experimental Evidence and Hypothesis', *AG Nerv Super*, 25, 110-120, (1983).
2. Williams, R.B., Lane, J.D., Kuhn, C.M., *et. al.*, 'Type A Behaviour and Elevated Physiological and Neuroendocrine Responses to Cognitive Tasks', *Science*, 218, 483-485, (1982).
3. Verrier, L.L., Hagestad, E.L., Lown, B., 'Delayed Myocardial Ischaemia Induced by Anger', *Circulation*, 75, 1. 249-254, (1987).
4. Leavitt, F., Garron, D.C., Blelauskas, L.A., 'Stressing Life Events and the Experience of Low Back Pain', *J Psychosom Res*, 23, 49-55, (1979).
5. Whitehead, W.E., Schuster, M.M., *Gastrointestinal Disorders, Behavioural and Physiological Basis for Treatment*, Academic Press, London, 1985.

Chapter 7

References

1. Patel, C. et al, 'Trial of relaxation in reducing coronary risk: 4-year follow-up', *BMJ* 290, (1985), 1103-6.

2. Barber, T.X., 'Physiological effects of hypnosis', *Psychological Bulletin* 58, (1961), 390–419.

Further reading

Benson, H., *The Relaxation Response*, (William Morrow & Co., Inc., New York, 1975).

Everly, G.S. Jr., Rosenfeld, R., *The Nature and Treatment of the Stress Response*, (Plenum Press, New York, 1981).

Bowers, K., *Hypnosis for the Seriously Curious*, (Brooks/Cole, Monterey, California, 1976).

Jacobson, E., *You Must Relax*, (McGraw-Hill, New York, 1978).

Soskis, D.A., *Teaching Self-Hypnosis: An Introductory Guide for Clinicians*, (W.W. Norton, New York, 1986).

Altman, B.H., Lambrou, P.T., 'Self-Hypnosis: A Complete Manual for Health and Self-Change', (International Health Publications, San Diego, 1985).

Chapter 8

References

1. Wood, P.D., Terry, R.B. and Haskell, W.L., 'Metabolism of substates', *Diet, Lipoprotein Metabolism and Exercise Federation Proc.*, 44(2): 358, (1985).
2. Kiens, B., Lithell, H.L. and Vessby, B., 'Further increases in high density lipoprotein in trained males after endurance training', *Eur. J. Appl. Physiol*, 52: 426, (1984).
3. Brownell, K.D., Bachorik, P.S., and Ayerle, R.S., 'Changes in plasma lipid and lipoprotein levels in men and women after a program of moderate exercise', *Circulation*, 65: 477–84, (1982).
4. Langosch, W., 'Psychological effects of training in coronary patients: a critical review of the literature', *European Heart J.* 9 (Suppl M) 37–42, (1988).
5. Kearney, J.T., Stull, G.A., Ewing, J.L., Strein, J.W., 'Cardiorespiratory Responses of sedentary college women as a function of training intensity', *J. Appl. Physiol*, 41: 822, (1976).
6. Bouchard, C., Bouley, M., Thibault, M.C. et al, 'Training of submaximal working capacity: frequency, intensity, duration and their interactions', *J. Sports Med*, 20: 29–40 (1980).
7. Hollman, W., Rost, R., Liesen, H. et al, 'Assessment of different forms of physical activity with respect to preventive and rehabilitative cardiology', *Int. J. Sports Medicine*, 2: 67–80. (1981).

Further reading

Astrand, P., Rodahl, K., *Textbook of Work Physiology*, (McGraw-Hill Book Co., Singapore, 1986).

Julian, D.G., *Angina Pectoris*, (Churchill Livingstone, Edinburgh, 1985).

Fentem, P.H., Bassey, E.J., Turnbull, N.B., *The new case for exercise*, (UK Sports Council and Health Education Authority joint publication, 1988).

Exercise. Why bother? (UK Sports Council and Health Education Authority joint publication).

Chapter 9

References

1. Royal College of Physicians of London, *Health or smoking? Follow-up report of the Royal College of Physicians*, (Churchill Livingstone, Edinburgh, 1986).
2. Moczurad, K.W., Curylo, A.M. and Dubiel, J.P., 'Smoking cessation as the factor reducing the risk of reinfarction and sudden death in the five year follow-up studies', In M. Aoki, S. Hisamichi and S. Tominaga (eds), *Smoking and Health*, (Exerpta Medica, International Congress Series, 780; 1988).
3. Schwartz, J.L., *Review and evaluation of smoking cessation methods: the United States and Canada 1978-1985*, (U.S. Department of Health and Human Sciences, 1987).

Further reading

Bennett, P. and Clapham, M., *Kicking the Habit. How to stop smoking and stay stopped*, (Shadowfax, Cardiff, 1989).

Chapter 10

References

1. Keys, A., 'Coronary Heart Disease in Seven Countries', *Circulation* 41, 1-198 (1970).
2. Castelli, W.P., 'Epidemiology of Coronary Heart Disease: The Framingham Study', *JAMA* Feb 4-12 1982.
3. Dayton, S. et al, 'A Controlled clinical trial of a diet high in unsaturated fat in preventing complication of atherosclerosis'. *Circulation* 40 (supplement 11) 58-60 (1969).
4. Nikkila, E., 'Prevention of progression of coronary atherosclerosis by treatment of hyperlipidaemia: a seven year prospective angiographic study' *BMJ* 289 220-3 (1984).
5. Grundy, S.M., 'Rationale of the diet-heart statement of the American Heart Association: Report of Nutrition Committee', *Circulation* 65 839-45A (1982).
6. COMA, 'Diet and Cardiovascular Disease', DHSS Report (HMSO London, 1984).

Sources of further information

Many of these addresses are self-explanatory. The list also includes self-help support groups run by ex-heart patients for other heart patients, usually on a small informal group basis.

Action on Smoking and Health (ASH), 5–11 Mortimer Street, London W1N 7RH (Tel. (071) 737 9843).

The British Acupuncture Association and Register, 34 Alderney Street, London SW1.

British Cardiac Society, 7 St Andrew's Place, Regent's Park, London NW1 4LB (Tel. (071) 486 6430).

British Heart Foundation, 102 Gloucester Place, London W1H 4DH (Tel. (071) 935 0185).

The Chest, Heart and Stroke Association (CHSA), Tavistock House North, Tavistock Square, London WC1H 9JE (Tel. (071) 387 3012).

CHSA – Interheart, 60 Barry Road, Netherall, Leicester LE5 1FB (Tel. (0533) 431194).

Coronary Artery Research Disease Foundation (CORDA), Tavistock House North, Tavistock Square, London WC1H 9TH (Tel. (071) 387 9779).

The Coronary Prevention Group, 60 Great Ormond Street, London WC1N 3HR (Tel. (071) 833 3687).

Exercise Rehabilitation Association, Wellesley House, 117 Wellington Road, Dudley, West Midlands DY1 1UB (Tel. (0384) 230222).

Family Heart Association, P.O. Box 116, Kidlington, Oxford OX5 1DT (Tel. (08675) 79125).

Health Education Authority, Hamilton House, Mabledon Place, London WC1H 9TX (Tel. (071) 631 0930).

Heart Beat Wales, Brunel House, 2 Fitzallen Road, Cardiff CF2 1EB ('Tel. (0222) 472472)

Heart to Heart, P.O. Box 7, High Street, Kershaw, Worcester.

The Irish Heart Foundation, 4 Clyde Road, Dublin 4, Eire (Tel. (0001) 685 001).

Look After Yourself Project Centre, Christchurch College, Canterbury, Kent CT1 1QU.

National Council of Voluntary Organisations, 26 Bedford Square, London Tel. (071) 636 4066).

Northern Ireland CHSA, Bryson House, 28 Bedford Street, Belfast BT2 7FJ (Tel. (0232) 220 184).

The Sports Council, 16 Upper Woburn Place, London WC1H 0QP.

The Zipper Club, 64 Sherwood Way, West Wickham, Kent BR4 9PD (Tel. (081) 777 4944).

American Heart Association, 7320 Grenville Avenue, Dallas, Texas, 75231, USA.

American Psychological Association, 1200 17th St. NW, Washington DC, 20036, USA.

Australian National Heart Foundation:
343 Riley Street, Surrey Hills, 2010 NSW. Tel: (02) 211 5188
464 William Street, West Melbourne, 3003 VIC. Tel: (03) 329 8511
557 Gregory Terrace, Fortitude Valley, 4006 QLD. Tel: (07) 854 1696
155-159 Hutt Street, Adelaide, 5000 SA. Tel: (08) 223 3144
43 Stirling Highway, Nedlands, 6009 WA. (09) 386 8926
24 Cavenagh St, Darwin, 0700 NT. Tel: (089) 81 1966
86 Hampden Road, Battery Point, 7001 TAS. Tel: (002) 34 5330

Australian Psychological Association, Nat. Science Centre, 191 Royal Parade, Parkville, Victoria 3052, Australia.

Positive Heart Living, Victoria Health Centre, 65 Brunswick Street, Fredericton E3B 1G5, New Brunswick, Canada.

Pakistan National Heart Association, c/o Armed Forces Institute of Cardiology, Rawalpindi, Pakistan.

For a cassette tape copy of the relaxation exercises described in Chapter 7, send a s.a.e. enclosing a cheque for £8.00 payable to the Angina Research Group, 64 Woodfield Road, Kings Heath, Birmingham B13 9UJ.

Index